Angus&Robertson

AF865084

Twenty-seven-year-old Scotsman David Mackenzie Angus stepped ashore in Australia in 1882, hoping that the climate would improve his health. While working for a Sydney bookseller, he managed to save the grand sum of £50 – enough to open his very own second-hand bookshop. He hired fellow-Scot George Robertson and in 1886 Angus & Robertson was born.

They ventured into publishing in 1888 with a collection of poetry by H. Peden Steele, and by 1895 had a bestseller on their hands with A.B. 'Banjo' Paterson's *The Man from Snowy River and Other Verses.* A&R confirmed the existence of Australian talent – and an audience hungry for Australian content. The company went on to add some of the most famous names in Australian literature to its list, including Henry Lawson, Norman Lindsay, C.J. Dennis and May Gibbs. Throughout the twentieth century, authors such as Xavier Herbert, Ruth Park, George Johnston and Peter Goldsworthy continued this tradition.

The A&R Australian Classics series is a celebration of the many authors who have contributed to this rich catalogue of Australian literature and to the cultural identity of a nation.

These classics are our indispensable voices. At a time when our culture was still noisy with foreign chatter and clouded by foreign visions, these writers told us our own stories and allowed us to examine and evaluate both our homeplace and our place in the world. – GERALDINE BROOKS

About the Author

Kevin Gilbert was born in 1933 to the Wiradjuri nation in central New South Wales, the youngest of eight children. Orphaned at the age of seven, he quickly learnt what it meant to be black and poor in Australia. His early life included stints in orphanages, fruit picking, and returns to his mother's People living on their traditional lands. In 1957 he was sentenced to life imprisonment for the killing of his wife. He served fourteen and a half years in Her Majesty's prisons.

Kevin Gilbert educated himself in prison, where he developed his poetic skills and became a dramatist, writer and an accomplished artist in oils and lino cut. He used these abilities to demonstrate to white Australians the injustice and inhumanity shown towards his People. Kevin fought for Aboriginal rights throughout his life, joining the Gurindji campaign and establishing the idea of the Aboriginal Tent Embassy in Canberra, in 1972. He became chairman of the 'Treaty 88' campaign, which aimed to build a proper foundation for the people of Australia.

His numerous published works indicate his status as a leading literary and political figure. His play *The Cherry Pickers* is the first play written by an Aboriginal person, and *Because A White Man'll Never Do It* is the first major political work by an Aboriginal person. Kevin's literary talents have become increasingly recognised and acknowledged — his oral history *Living Black* won the National Book Council Award in 1978, and in 1988 he was awarded the Human Rights Award for Literature for his anthology *Inside Black Australia,* but he refused the award, on the grounds that Aboriginal People still awaited their basic human rights in their own land. In 1992 he received a four-year Creative Fellowship for his 'outstanding contribution to the nation'. Kevin Gilbert died in April 1993 aged fifty-nine.

To find out more, visit the author's website:
www.kevingilbert.com.au

Also by Kevin Gilbert

The Cherry Pickers 1968
Poems 1969
End of Dream-time 1971
Living Black: Blacks Talk to Kevin Gilbert 1977
People Are Legends 1978
Inside Black Australia: An Anthology of Aboriginal Poetry 1988
Aboriginal Sovereignty: Justice, the Law and Land 1988
Child's Dreaming (with Eleanor Williams) 1992
Black from the Edge (with Eleanor Williams) 1994
Me and Mary Kangaroo 1994

BECAUSE A WHITE MAN'LL NEVER DO IT

KEVIN GILBERT

A&R

AUSTRALIAN CLASSICS

A&R Classics
An imprint of HarperCollins*Publishers,* Australia

First published in Australia in 1973
by Angus & Robertson Publishers
This edition published in 2013
by HarperCollins*Publishers* Pty Limited
ABN 36 009 913 517
harpercollins.com.au

HarperCollinsPublishers
Macken House, 39/40 Mayor Street Upper
Dublin 1, D01 C9W8, Ireland

HarperCollins *Publishers*
Level 13, 201 Elizabeth Street, Sydney NSW 2000, Australia
31 View Road, Glenfield, Auckland 10, New Zealand
A 53, Sector 57, Noida, UP, India
77-85 Fulham Palace Road, London W6 8JB, United Kingdom
2 Bloor Street East, 20th floor, Toronto, Ontario M4W 1A8, Canada
10 East 53rd Street, New York NY 10022, USA

National Library of Australia Cataloguing-in-Publication data:

Gilbert, Kevin, 1933–1993 author.
Because a white man'll never do it.
ISBN 978 0 7322 9730 5 (pbk.)
ISBN 978 1 7430 9990 2 (ebook)
A&R Australian classics.
Aboriginal Australians – Government policy.
Aboriginal Australians – Treatment of.
Aboriginal Australians – Civil rights.
323.119915

Original cover design by Darren Holt, HarperCollins Design Studio,
adapted by Natalie Winter
Cover image © Kellie Block/Newspix
Typeset in 10.5/12pt Times by Kirby Jones
Printed and bound in Australia by McPhersons Printing Group
The papers used by HarperCollins in the manufacture of this book are a natural, recyclable product made from wood grown in sustainable plantation forests. The fibre source and manufacturing processes meet recognised international environmental standards, and carry certification.

5 4 3 2 1 13 14 15 16

This book is dedicated to the Aboriginal patriots of Australia who have refused to sell out, have refused to pay that ultimate 'price of survival' demanded by the white boss … and to the mass of blacks, 'poor buggars all', who are still waiting …

PUBLISHER'S NOTE

This edition preserves Kevin Gilbert's text as first published in 1973. It includes some words and phrases such as 'half-castes' and 'full bloods', which are no longer considered appropriate or relevant, due to their divisive nature.

WARNING: This book contains names of people who have passed on.

Foreword

Humane persons such as Martin Luther King, Malcolm X, Oodgeroo Noonuccal and Kevin Gilbert share a central vision of a healing process which extends from the spiritual, through the social milieu of their people, to a positive future in which old wounds are healed and a new day of a common humanity dawns, pregnant with possibilities. They rise above personal adversities to formulate and communicate their vision. I place Kevin Gilbert among the visionaries of this world because he sought throughout his life to change the quality of life for all people in Australia. It is a sad state of affairs, a problem with the overall cultural matrix of Australia that such men and women are allowed to remain on the fringes of the mainstream, that instead of being taken into the hearts of all Australians and treated as national treasures, they are ignored, or seemingly ignored. I say 'seemingly' because I have taken out a copy of *Because A White Man'll Never Do It* from the library of Murdoch University and note that since 1987 over fifty people have borrowed the book. Does this mean that his message is getting through to many people, and that his influence is growing steadily in segments of the mainstream Australian community? I expect that we'll have to wait and see, while those with lesser things to say have their hour upon the stage.

Kevin Gilbert has always been an influential writer and thinker among Aboriginal People. I remember being at the First

Black Playwrights Conference and Workshop held in Canberra in 1987, when Kevin put on his play *The Cherry Pickers* with a newly written prologue part of which was in blank verse. It was given a standing ovation by the audience. The prologue was an account of Aboriginal genesis and an early stage of happiness which ended abruptly, leaving only the hope of an eventual return from conditions set out in the rest of the drama. Kevin, it must be remembered, was the first Aborigine to write a play. He was a forerunner in most of his work, which was not divorced from his People, but utilised tape recordings and anthologies of Aboriginal writings to get the message across. He was not a solitary man writing from within a solitary vision, but, rather, he was closely in tune and in contact with the hopes and aspirations of his People.

It was a sad day when Kevin passed from our midst and he will be sorely missed; but he has left behind a corpus of work, which is scathing in its condemnation of man's inhumanity to man, as well as being a call for a new deal for Australia's indigenous minority. It is easy to condemn the present and difficult to present a vision of the future. In this book, though published in 1973 in the heady days of the Whitlam era, Kevin Gilbert wrote about the problems which still plague Australia and Aboriginal affairs today. It is not enough to declare that Aboriginal problems are health, education and employment and when these are fixed so will be the problem. Such policies hide the fact that there is a political dimension that must also be addressed; but not from the top down. Kevin Gilbert was scathing in his criticism of governments throwing money at Aboriginal problems without taking into consideration the blight of the soul caused by a history of massacre and racial genocide. This too has to be addressed, but first it must be accepted that there is a political problem and that this demands a political solution. It is not enough to set up from above a reconciliation council, put on it a few Jackies and then fling out some money for a few television advertisements. Such reconciliation in Post-Mabo Australia is a travesty that must be put to rest.

Mabo may be seen either as a victory for Aboriginal People, or a defeat; but what we must remember is that Native Title has been recognised and that this may be used as a springboard to a more widespread political solution. In fact, the High Court decision really was an acceptance of the historical position taken in Kevin's book, and now is the time for his words on the future of Australia to be taken into account. In 1987 Kevin Gilbert helped to draft a comprehensive treaty which he first published that year. This important document could form the basis of laying to rest both the ghost of reconciliation and the various Mabo legislation messes. If reconciliation is to be successful it must be from negotiations directly entered into between representatives of the Aboriginal People and the Australian government. Such negotiations can use documents like Kevin's draft treaty as frames of reference in setting the Aboriginal agenda. The negotiations may take years, a lifetime, but then whatever progress Aborigines have made has occurred over the lifetime of Kevin Gilbert. We have all the time necessary to effect a just and true reconciliation, one which is not foisted on us from Canberra. It is often asked what Aborigines want and then answered with a shrug. The fact is answers have been provided by Aboriginal writers such as Kevin Gilbert that are simply ignored by those in power.

I may sound too political in this foreword, but then this book is one of the best political books on land rights ever written in Australia, and is a call to action and a galvanisation of the People. It is a hard act to follow, or even introduce. It is a sad book too, because although published in 1973, it is still so awfully relevant to us. It has been said that those who ignore history are forced to repeat it, and the short history of Australia has been a constant repetition of government policies imposed on Aboriginal People from above. If you don't believe this read *Because A White Man'll Never Do It.* This book has now achieved its majority being first published twenty-one years ago; but Aboriginal lives are still ordered and governed by a bureaucracy from Canberra. It is timely that this book is being republished, what with the continuing debate on Native Title and the push for reconciliation. This book is for both Aborigines and non-Aborigines and I end this foreword with

Kevin's closing words, before he intervened with an epilogue written while he was correcting the proofs. An epilogue which forecasts the position of Aboriginal affairs in 1994.

The human metals melt and melting down
Strike fault in fault and shattering neath the steel
The two base metals scream a new appeal.

Kevin Gilbert is now gone from us and our country is poorer for his absence; but his words live on. Read them and find an original and Aboriginal thinker who wrote from the heartlands of the Australian spirit.

MUDROOROO,
MARCH 1994

Author's Note

A recent book by a white man on the subject of Aboriginal affairs (and a good one it was too) indicated the author's gratitude to a petroleum company for providing the means for the author's travel to research his book. Books by white people on black subjects seem to be very much in fashion lately. There also seems to be unlimited funds for study grants, research projects and the setting up of commissions to study that most 'in' subject — Aboriginal affairs. With a few glad exceptions, these efforts never get to the core of the Aboriginal soul, for what the black man says is one thing, what he feels is another and the white interpretation is generally yet another. Of course I, as an Aboriginal, am not 'qualified' to undertake any of the research projects into Aboriginal affairs — I never made sixth class primary school. (Not that I would want to undertake research anyway — it seems to me that there has long been too damn much research and not enough action.)

So I too, must give my thanks — to those Aboriginal people who gave interviews which became part of the subject matter of this book. Besides that, I am indebted to nobody. Black writers don't seem to get very much support from either government or big companies. Perhaps they feel that whites can do it better? Or are they afraid that too accurate a black view will come through?

*

Looking at the manuscript at the proof stage and comparing it with my original draft I am amused to see how much has had to be left out because *truth is libel* in New South Wales. Several of the incidents and examples that I originally quoted had to be deleted because, as the publisher sadly said 'some of "them" would just *love* to have a go'. So for the protection both of myself and my publishers, parts of the book have, perhaps, lost some of the punch they originally had and some of the main actors in the drama have got off rather lightly in the weighing scales of history.

During the final stages of the preparation of this book the Literature Board announced that I had been awarded a half year fellowship. So I must give thanks after all. The money will go some way towards re-paying the debts that I incurred during the writing of it.

1973

Introduction

Changes in Aboriginal affairs are happening at such a fast pace, these days, that I have no doubt that by the time this book comes out, a lot of the fine detail will have changed. But fine detail, veneer, is one thing and the unchanging core of hard facts underneath is quite another. I do not think that the gut things will have changed very much and that is what this book is mostly about.

Also, I am acutely aware that the book must incorporate some straight errors of fact, incomplete information and information that was dated at the time when I used it. There are probably errors that I am unaware of or only half aware of — for example, as I write this Introduction, just before the book goes to the printer, I believe that the situation at the Walgett Foundation of Aboriginal Affairs has changed somewhat, although I do not know in what way. I would have liked to have done many more interviews than I was able to do and I would have liked to have got them from all over Australia, including from the tribal blacks. But I do not any longer have the means to do the necessary travelling — my days of roving reportage are over. That was part of the reason why my magazine, *Alchuringa*, which some readers may remember, is pretty well dead. Poor little *Alchu* always did have all the cards stacked against her, although, God knows, she tried. And of course the magazine was hopelessly New South Wales-centred, for obvious reasons. So is this book. And yet it is not, for the main themes with which it deals are themes that are vital and central to the thinking of every aware black in Australia. Another thing. It is no use, when reporting on Aboriginal affairs, to breeze in, interview someone and breeze out again. (That is why you see such howlers in the newspapers at times.) Because often the politics behind the facts cast a very different complexion on things. So you have to hang around for a while, questioning blacks, watching blacks, to get at the truth. It helps, of course, if you are black yourself.

An obvious white man's criticism against this book will be that it is not representative. Of course it isn't, because nearly all the people whom I interviewed for it are (or were) activists in some way or another. But as I said before, the main themes are deep in the hearts and minds of Aborigines. The *comments* about these themes may be a little ahead of their time, considering where the average black in this country now stands, but they are the shadow of things to come, a genesis of black political thinking.

I have read the two poems that form the introduction to the last chapter to various Aborigines, mostly women, and have been sad to note that it is the negative poem, 'Grandmother Koori', that gets the best response. It is a response of bitter amusement, of race/self-deprecation. How our people lean to the negative as a conditioned response! Of course the men tended more towards the second poem, 'Grandfather Koori', not so much for the hope that it holds out but because it provides some salve for wounded pride. But whether your tastes run to the negative or to the positive, the book should provide enough meat to keep students of Aboriginal affairs thinking.

And the black participants, too. I believe there is enough here to keep Kooris studying, debating, agreeing, disagreeing. Probably what many of them say about it will be one thing and what they know in their hearts will be another. Perhaps some Kooris will want to come and give me a punch in the nose (although they won't actually get around to doing it). A good few blacks aren't going to like seeing themselves reflected, warts and all, in the pages of this book. Blacks are no more fond of home truths than any other human beings. Yet truth has a sort of irresistibility. You've got to keep coming back to it in order to see clearly where you're at, where you are going and of course, what you are. There can't be any growth without it.

This book pretty well marks my swan-song in Aboriginal affairs, which fact brings me some regrets and a lot of relief. Writing a book, it turns out, is all I *can* do in Aboriginal affairs. I remember last year having a talk with a grizzled, life-stained, battered old black man leaning against a fence on the outskirts of Coonamble. I don't remember his exact words but they boiled down to the question, 'What, besides a lot of bullshit that got *him* a good job, has Charlie Perkins ever really done for you or me?' It may or may not have been a fair question but what the old man didn't realise was that a fairer one still would have been, 'What, with all the best will in the world, *could* he do?' The same thing applies to every other individual, white or black. All individuals can do in the final analysis is stir. But you get a bit sick of stirring because it is so constantly negative. So I have written this book in an attempt not just to stir, but to stimulate the thinking of both white people and black people in this country. It is based on personal knowledge, many discussions with Aborigines all over New South Wales, tape-recorded interviews, newspaper clippings and quotes from various magazines and journals. I believe that it could profitably be read by Aborigines, even slowly, haltingly, tortuously, on the reserves (a 'Little Black Book'?). But of course it won't get to them, bar the odd, stray copy, because nothing like that ever does.

Blacks are supposed to be getting a new deal now and there are signs that this might be at least partially true. But black people remember that Frederick Douglass, the American Negro ex-slave and freedom fighter, speaking in 1849 said, 'Find out just what people will submit to and you have found out the exact amount of injustice and wrong which will be imposed upon them.' The whites have another saying, 'The pen is mightier than the sword.' Shall we see then, shall we, which of the two statements rings truest?

K. J. G.
1973

Contents

I

Race Memories

EARTH

Of the earth am I
The breast that nurtured all the young
Of earth; with earth to earth again I fly
With every thought I thought and song I sung
Was earth and earth in all its bounty
Gave to me and mine a wise increase.

I am earth; and when the first ship came
They spat and cursed the earth as foul base
Most miserable of all the earth was I
Without the spice or wine of their much wiser race.

The learned came; and said Gods had I none
But totems and an animism dull
There was no high god somewhere in the sky
No higher metaphysics in my lower type of skull.

I am earth; missionaries looked askance
Upon my nature undisguised: my earthy lance
Was to them unclean; a blight to God
And such disgusting things hide from His sight.

Of the earth am I; benighted anthropologists
Wont to declare: The basest of the base and by their skull
No glimmer of intelligence is there
They measured vacuity to fill their empty space.

I am earth; my God, my High God had I one
Ba'aime, though I did not know the high
And separate classes making God apart
From me and spirit beings who did his will.

Of the earth am I; the high God ne'er considered
That he was far too high to dwell with me
Together, as he breathed so breathed I
Together, to the hunt, was he and I
Together walked we two on earth

And sometimes in the sky.
The learned came; and said gods had I none
No politics nor sovereign embassy
Their learned ignorance served as a pass
For pioneers to kill the god in me.

Ever since the invasion of our country by English soldiers and then colonists in the late eighteenth century, Aborigines have endured a history of land theft, attempted racial extermination, oppression, denial of basic human rights, actual and de facto slavery, ridicule, denigration, inequality and paternalism. Concurrently, we suffered the destruction of our entire way of life — spiritual, emotional, social and economic. The result is the Aboriginal of twentieth century Australia — a man without hope or happiness, without a land, without an identity, a culture or a future.

While the wooden weapons of the Aboriginal tribes of Australia were no match against the musketry of the white invaders — whose invasion was, therefore, relatively easily accomplished — it is a point of pride to black Australians today that history documents the widespread resistance of the

Aboriginal tribes against the squatters' inroads on their land. At best, black resistance kept whites out of certain areas for some years longer than would otherwise have been the case. These areas were, for a while longer at least, 'blackfeller country'. At worst, black resistance provoked the punitive raids, massacres and mass poisonings that remain branded in the race memory of every Aboriginal in Australia today.

Estimates suggest that in 1788 there were some 300,000 Aborigines who roamed their tribal areas in family groups, coming together periodically as tribes to carry out their increase ceremonies, initiation rituals and so forth. Some tribes numbered several hundred while others had as many as a thousand or more. Anyone who trespassed onto another tribe's land except on recognised business was in danger of attack. The inheritance of land was a totally secure, neverending state of possession that extended generation after generation to all those born within the material and spiritual boundaries of their tribal area. Each member of the tribe had his rights and responsibilities — the right to sustenance from the land and responsibility for its ritual upkeep. Food taboos ensured that no birds, plants or animals were too heavily hunted — a type of natural conservation that helped preserve the balance of nature. There were no fences or boundaries in the European sense, but each tribal area was clearly defined by landmarks such as mountain ranges, rocks, trees and waterholes which all had a rich cultural and spiritual significance for the people. Within these landmarks dwelt the spirits and totem gods that nourished, protected and gave continuing life to the owners of that tribal area.

In the English tradition, land titles were originally granted by the Crown, after which they became transferable. The Aboriginal title was in perpetuity and was inalienably held by a group of people. As land was not merely a source of sustenance but also a living spiritual entity, an inextricable part of the life of the tribe, the question of transfer or barter could never arise, for this would have implied the bartering of the very soul sustenance, the Dreaming, which would have been tantamount to suicide for the tribe. Not only did the land belong to them, but they belonged to it — now and forever. They had belonged to it in the past, the now and in the future when they would die and return again in spirit and in substance to their Dreaming-place. That is why it was impossible for white squatters to 'buy' or 'take' the land, although they could, with the sanction of the tribe, use it, share in its bounty and become part of the pattern of life.

The tribes had led a nomadic life through necessity because there were not plants or animals suitable for domestication. To maintain a balanced diet the people had to keep on the move, seeking the quondong here, the kangaroo there, emus, wild ducks, honey, fish, nardoo in other places. Within a generation of their arrival in New South Wales, the invaders had made such an impact upon the ecology of the land that Charles Darwin, reporting on what he saw in 1836 in *The Voyage of the Beagle* wrote:

> A few years since this country abounded with wild animals; but now the emu is banished to a long distance and the kangaroo has become scarce; to both the English greyhound has been highly destructive. The numbers of Aborigines is rapidly decreasing. This decrease, no doubt must be partly owing to the introduction of spirits, to European diseases, even the milder ones of which, such as measles, prove very destructive, and to the gradual extinction of the wild animals. It is said that numbers of their children invariably perish in very early infancy from the effects of their wandering life, and, as the difficulty of procuring food increases, so must their wandering habits increase, and hence the population is repressed without any apparent deaths from famine ... The offal, when a beast is killed, and some milk from the cows are the peace offerings of the settlers.

When resistance to the white invaders proved fruitless against the continuing usurpation of Aboriginal territory, many tribes tried to withdraw to the furthest points of their land. But they found that the natural economy could not sustain their inroads on the more restricted area. As a result, hunger forced them back into the white settled areas to spear sheep and cattle and to pilfer from the shepherds' huts. Then settlers began to leave them poisoned flour in the huts — flour laced with strychnine — in an attempt to wipe out the black 'nuisance'. Aboriginal leaders tried to organise their spears against the muskets of the settlers. Where they met with some success, history records the 'atrocities of the blacks'. There are numerous testimonies to the white man's retaliatory and punitive sabre charges against the tribesmen, women and children. 'Boong fires' destroyed the bodies of the troublemakers. Individual Aboriginal men were killed and their women and children raped, then shot. Young children, considered 'safe' venereal disease risks, were raped. Consider events such as the Namoi River massacre. The Coniston killings. The Murrumbidgee River wipeout. The black extermination drives of the Hawkesbury and Manning Rivers. The genocide of the Tasmanian blacks. These and many, many more were the links in the chain of white inhumanity that lives on in the memories of the southern part-bloods today.

Aborigines became, officially, a dying race. The tribes were divided from each other as individuals were forcibly transported to strange areas where they had no tribal affiliations or spiritual landmarks. Others died in police lock-ups. Some cried for Christ, and, by submitting to the directions of their Christian 'brothers', received some sort of welcome — not, in view of the extreme racist prejudices of the day, in terms of human equality, but, well, they were allowed to live. Once the niceties of civilised behaviour were established it was but a short step to introduce habit-forming substances such as tobacco, alcohol and a taste for sugar and tea which quickly brought about an almost total dependence on whites for handouts. To sustain the goodwill that kept the handouts coming, blacks found that they had to work — as prostitutes without fee, as stockmen without pay — a virtual slavery. Concurrently, the white race found it necessary also to demean and ridicule the tribal identity of Aborigines. They said that blacks were ignorant, heathen, savages without a technology, a government or an organisation. The transfer of their attitudes and values to their black servants led to intense feelings of shame on the part of the blacks. Much of this shame survives today. It can be seen in the poetry of Kath Walker who, though feeling that her ancestors were inferior to the clever white man, nevertheless struggles to identify herself with the underdog.

Price of survival. Bewildered by the strange new conditions of life, the Aborigine bowed to his forced removal from his tribal area even though he knew that if he were to die in a strange area his spirit would be lost forever. He bowed to the ward system by which the various authorities could split families and assign him, his wife or his children to separate areas as servant-slaves to white squatters. He bowed to the apartheid-style policies that kept him apart on reserves. He bowed to the nightly curfews that kept him out of towns. He bowed to segregation rules of hospitals that ensured that his kind would not receive proper medical attention or humane care. He bowed to the power exercised by squatters on the stations over every facet of his life, diet and actions. He bowed to the demands of stockmen and squatters for 'black velvet'. He bowed to the fact of his women having to prostitute themselves for the food that would allow the children to survive, or for the alcohol that would yield the oblivion that was so much more desirable than daily reality. In the end, shamefully, he bowed to the fact that his children were doomed to die in anguish from the starvation that his women could no longer avert, or the diseases which the white man had introduced and now did nothing to check. For a long time it was indeed believed that his race was doomed. Extermination campaigns, detribalisation, denigration, exploitation; many, many factors pointed to the impending death of a people. And as a pure race, southern blacks did die. But the half-castes increased, thanks to the propensity of the master race, Australia's proud pioneering stock, to lie with the despised blacks. Thanks to the urge to visit the blacks' camps by night, seeking the titillation and human warmth denied them between the cold starched sheets at home.

Came the government reserves and the mission settlements where the white manager was placed over the blacks as virtual dictator. Where, if it pleased him, he supplied them with government rations. Such was the power of the manager's rule, backed as he was by police power, that he indeed had blacks eating out of his hands. All these factors combined to leave the Aboriginal psyche shattered, ripped, tattered. A black man became a thing to joke about. No longer a mighty hunter, his personality had become so crippled that he could no longer either fight for his human entitlements or work for them. So he became a stockman without pay or a mission black on government rations or a cringing shadow on the street that cadged off whites for a feed and a bottle of plonk.

Not only did the Aborigine lose his pride, his place and his identity but group distinctions began to intrude to complicate the situation yet further. The mission blacks were taught by missionaries to deny their 'animal nature'. Fundamentalist rectitude locked young blacks, male and female, in separate dormitories to save them from themselves. There they stayed, in these prison-like dormitories, at all times except in class hours or prayer meetings, until the youngsters were well past marriageable age and had been so indoctrinated against their 'unclothed heathen' brothers that they accepted their new lot in return, perhaps, for eventual salvation. On the other hand the tribally identified remnants sneered at these imitation blacks who bashed the bible to please the white fornicator who 'controlled their animal nature' but rarely his own.

The half-caste suffered on all fronts. In some places he was forcibly removed from his tribal parents by white authority. He was victimised by the churches who saw in him living proof, often, of the lust and hypocrisy of their members. The full-bloods disowned him because he was a 'yellah feller' tainted with the white, murderous blood. So the distinctions increased — the distinctions between government reserve blacks, church blacks, fringe-dwelling blacks and part-assimilated town blacks who looked down on what they regarded as their more backward brothers.

Even today the northern full-bloods do not consider that the southern blacks are Aborigines, although a Pan-Aboriginal feeling is on the move. The one fact on which all blacks — full-blood and part-blood, tribal and detribalised — meet, is the shared fact of persecution by whites. All share the hatred and the overwhelming realisation of the enormity of white racial injustice; this is the cement that binds all blacks in unity. Read the testimony of Pincher Numiari, a Gurindji elder telling the story of the arrival of the white man to his land. Then read the testimony of a southern part-Aboriginal woman, tape-recorded last year. Their experience is very different and yet very similar. Their burden is the same — the white man.

Said Pincher Numiari to a member of the Gurindji Campaign:

> White European was coming in. He was first come from Sydney. He coming in through Queensland to Wave Hill Station. He went over here to Black Gin. He pick that place first when he first come but he change his mind and he came right to Victoria River and he found a place over there. And he bring the horses, a few horses and he had a bullock wagon. The Aborigines, they been quiet. They [the whites] been found them Aborigines and shot him down here in Black Fellows Knob [pointing to a hill that can be seen from Wattie Creek]. I don't know how many men and women, kids got shot over there. I think we'll call that 'burial ground' bye and bye, because a lot of blokes got killed. They been shot by Europeans.
>
> They were just walking around hunting, you know. They been hunting for their own tucker, bush tucker.
>
> Poor old buggers, we didn't do nothing.
>
> When I been working around West Kimberleys, they been tell me same story, right back to Alice Springs, right back to Darwin, all those places, they tell the same story. They shot him down like a dog, same way like Gurindji. See that hill there, they been shot there. See that river, they been shot there ... They [the Aborigines] didn't know, poor buggers. They didn't know, because white Europeans never explained to them. Because when they found Aborigines they shot him like a dog straightaway.

> He didn't give him a fair go. Now this time we stand up and fight, we mob. We turn around and fight it out, see. We walk off that Wave Hill Station. They treat him like a dog. People was having a rough time. I don't know why that. When they first come, they been living cross-ways, and they been just walk over to married mens' camp and just take the girls away from Aborigines, and take her to Wave Hill Station, and they keep him [her] in bed. Tomorrow morning they let him [her] back to camp for their right husband, see. This what they been do when they first come. The white European been start it first, not Aborigine.
>
> (*by courtesy of The Gurindji Campaign*)

Said Alice Briggs, half a continent away from the Gurindji camp and several generations ahead of Pincher Numiari in experience of the effects of colonisation:

> The tribal people … they were strict in their ways. Not like a white man's law; it stinks, it does. And they've built these houses [at Purfleet Aboriginal Reserve near Taree, New South Wales], they put 'em here … instead of putting them here; why didn't they mind their own business and let Aborigines cater for themselves? That's how it should have been done. But they've ruined them and the neglect is not on the part of the Aborigine because it's a white man that's put it on 'em. He's made our men lazy, he's made our women what they are and everything that goes with it — and it's all come from a white man.
>
> The only answer is to give them back their land rights and let the Aborigine try and rectify what the white man has done, because a white man'll *never* do it. While ever he tries to tell an Aborigine what to do you're going to have the same thing all the way through life. And I for one don't want to see my kids grow up in the conditions that I've grown up in. And if the children of tomorrow are going to have a chance, it's not going to come from

education. Certainly not. It's got to be handed back to our people to educate their kids in their *own* way — and educate themselves. And make a life for themselves — but not to be hounded by a white man and be told to do it, because he *won't* do it.

It's this … now they've come out here, they've taken Australia and it's more or less as though they've taken us! That's where it is! Now look, everybody owns a piece of Australia. Now look at the miles and miles of land that's not being used. Why can't we have that? Why does the government own it? What did they do to own it? They came out here and they landed in one spot and they took the whole of Australia. Where does that leave us? We're just campin' on a white feller's reserve — that's all we're doing! And that's it. I don't really hate white people. I think all people should be equal. But not a white man to think he's God, or somebody, and you're the devil himself … because that's how they think of us, most white people do …

The people have nothing going for them here. The women have nothing. The kids have nothing. They go over town, they go pinching fruit and, believe me, they even as much as go and grub in the garbage cans — eating out of a garbage can! And the kids here, they really got nothing! Nothing for 'em and no one gives a damn and least of all the welfare officer that's supposed to be here helping the children! And little kids running over the street while their parents are in town.

There's your neglect, and there it is, brought on by a bloody white man — and that's right from the horse's mouth! And I'll tell even the Prime Minister of Australia the same thing. I've *seen* the little children for myself … and that's why it's got to come from us. We've got to help these kids out here ourselves … because as the magistrate said, the children out here are delinquents! Well, there it is, that's your problem. And it's not only *my* problem, it's everyone's around here, but the biggest majority around

> here haven't got the guts to stand up and say it! I'm a bundle of nerves, but by Jesus, I'll stand up for my kids and I think everybody else could do the same! ... Because I've been mother and father to my kids. I've reared my three kids from babies and I've had a bloody hard battle to rear my family ... and I'm not going to just sit back like some of 'em do and wonder how the kids are going to get through the next generation ... whether they're going to go on as second-class human beings all their life!

Both speakers carry the burden of the white man. Both carry in their mind the memory and the experience of his immorality, killing, rape and land theft. As a child of fourteen, I remember how my guts twisted with bitterness as I dug the skeletons of black women and children out of the sands of the Murrumbidgee and examined the squashed and bullet-riddled skulls. Many black families have some story, some horror story of racial massacre in their district. It is not that long ago that the last 'shoot-ups' occurred in blacks' camps — the local whites having themselves some fun. It's not that long ago that Aborigines were roped off in picture houses from the rest of the audience, that they couldn't get service in cafes etc. In some areas it still goes on. In more recent times, the figures on the number of black babies dying in the outback were ignored while this country gave generous millions to nations like Pakistan. Blacks know this. They know how little time has elapsed since they were not counted in the census. They lived through the shame of being 'second class' people in a country that denied them the right to social services, the right to walk into the country's lowest institutions, the pubs. Very few blacks have any land security as yet. Police victimisation and disadvantages before the law are attested to by the enormous disproportion of blacks in jail.

White man, you may well speak to the Aborigine of your 'democracy' and 'justice' and 'Christianity'. But your reality is a little at variance with your theory. The Aborigine snarls his disbelief of your words as he slinks away unmanned. Often he holds silence, for such is the beggarly state that society and circumstance have reduced him to — and this includes the 'respectable' blacks who have been singled out for white favour — that he will fawn obsequiously at your lies and half-truths. Once his fathers were men. Now he hopes, by fawning, to remain reasonably agreeable in your sight so that he may beg from you, borrow, or if he is one of the favoured ones, be given a more lucrative sinecure tomorrow. Underneath it all there is frustration, obsequious resentment, divided loyalties, uncertain values. There is no real belonging, no real identification except to the memory of misery. It is true that the modern Aborigine is sick, very sick. But let no white person use this as an excuse to denigrate him even further. You cannot look down on black people while you understand the historical reasons that have reduced them to what they are — the reasons of which I have here sketched only a tiny, general, impressionistic fraction. Remember that the Aborigine's sickness has been forced upon him. Yours you not only tolerate, but structure into the very fibres of your society.

2

People Speaking Out

LOVE? COUNTRY PARTY STYLE

Johnny boy was a nice, nice man
All soft an' bought me nice nice clothes
Me name is 'Mary' most call me 'Gin'
But Johnny the whiteman called me 'Rose'
He owned this place — Quondong station
Had his white wife lived in town
Couldn't marry — but he loved me
How his wife would scowl and frown
When he smiled at me and winked at me
With one eye and called me Rose
And I loved him yes I loved him loved him truly I
suppose
He was in the Country Party
All the people gave their vote
On his ticket, winning ticket
'I love Johnny' what I wrote
Signed it Rose, in brackets 'Mary'
Soon my Johnny came to power
He was KING of Aborigine
And Affairs — soon come my hour
Then I bore his blue-eyed baby

> 'Bout the time he made new Act
> That took half-castes off the blackgins
> Lost me baby, that's a fact!
> Come and took it like a chicken
> Like a calf took it away
> An' they called the new Act 'Welfare'
> And they took me child away.
>
> There's no white men, or woman, who has that feeling we have. They can study us all they like, but we've got them studied too. Because this is *our* country — the country of my mother's mother, a full-blooded Australian Aborigine. And it is *my* country. Always remember this. My Australian Aborigines did not go to England and claim it and then leave a whole lot of mixed bloods who no one wants. It is *our* country. It belongs to us, it is precious to us. And that is something no white man will ever understand, except perhaps Bill Harney and Don McLeod. They understood a little bit of what we feel and what we are.
>
> *Pearl Gibbs, seventy-two-year-old*
> *Aboriginal patriot, July '72*

Regrettably, given our present level of human evolution, 'human rights' tend still to be accorded to minority groups according to their capacity to demand same. Hence, for most of this century and, indeed, since colonisation first began, Aboriginal people could literally rot while the major society around them was re-forming and re-shaping itself in various ways. Certainly Aborigines were 'done to' according to various fashions ranging from annihilation to 'protection' (when it was thought they would die out) to 'assimilation/welfare' and so forth, but they pretty largely remained a passive group once the tribes' initial resistance had been broken. Only individuals such as Bill Ferguson, Pearl Gibbs and Bert Groves from the 'thirties in New South Wales, and similar Aboriginal identities in other states, raised their voices in protest. In 1941 Michael Sawtell, a member of the Aborigines Welfare Board, arranged for Pearl Gibbs to broadcast an appeal on behalf of her people. It was broadcast over radio 2GB by courtesy of the Theosophical Society in Sydney:

Good evening listeners,

I wish to express my deepest gratitude to the Theosophical Society of Sydney in granting me this privilege of being on the air this evening. It is the first time in the history of Australia that an Aboriginal woman has broadcast an appeal for her people. I am more than happy to be that woman. My grandmother was a full-blood Aborigine. Of that fact I am most proud. The admixture of white blood makes me a quarter-caste Aborigine. I am a member of the Committee for Aboriginal Citizenship.

My people have had 153 years of the white man's and white woman's cruelty and injustice and unchristian treatment imposed upon us. My race is fast vanishing. There are only 800 full-bloods now in New South Wales due to the maladministration of previous governments. However, intelligent and educated Aborigines, with the aid of good white friends, are protesting against these conditions. I myself have been reared independently of the Aborigines Protection Board now known as the Aborigines Welfare Board. I have lived and worked amongst white people all my life. I've been in close contact with Aborigines and I have been on Aboriginal stations in New South Wales for a few weeks and months at a time. I often visit them. Therefore I claim to have a thorough knowledge of both the Aboriginal and white viewpoints. I know the difference between the status of Aborigines and white men. When I say 'white man' I mean white women also. There are different statuses for different castes. A person in whom the Aborigine blood predominates is not entitled to an old-age, invalid or returned soldier's pension. There are about thirty full-blooded returned men in this state whom I believe are not entitled to the old-age pension. A woman in whom the Aborigine blood predominates is not entitled to a baby bonus.

Our girls and boys are exploited ruthlessly. They are apprenticed out by the Aborigines Welfare Board at the shocking wage of a shilling to three and six per week pocket money and from two and six to six shillings per week is paid into a trust fund at the end of four years. This is done from fourteen years to the age of eighteen. At the end of four years a girl would, with pocket money and money from the trust, have earned £60 and a boy £90. Many girls have great difficulty in getting their trust money. Others say they have never been paid. Girls often arrive home with white babies. I do not know of one case where the Aborigines Welfare Board has taken steps to compel the white father to support his child. The child has to grow up as an unwanted member of an apparently unwanted race. Aboriginal girls are no less human than my white sisters. The pitiful small wage encourages immorality. Women living on the stations do not handle endowment money, but the managers write out orders. The orders are made payable to one store in the nearest town — in most cases a mixed drapery and grocery store. So you will see that in most cases the mother cannot buy extra meat, fruit or vegetables. When rations and blankets are issued to the children, the value is taken from the endowment money. The men work sixteen hours per week for rations worth five and sixpence. The bad housing, poor water supply, appalling sanitary conditions and the lack of right food, together with unsympathetic managers, make life not worth living for my unfortunate people.

It has now become impossible for many reasons for a full-blood to own land in his own country. On the government settlements and in camps around the country towns, the town people often object to our children attending the school that white children attend. This is the unkindest and cruellest action I know. Many of the white people call us vile names and say that our children are not fit to associate with white children. If this is so, then the white people must also take their share of the blame. I'm very concerned about the 194 full-blooded Aboriginal children left in this state. What is going to happen to them? Are you going to give them a chance to be properly educated and grow up as good Australian citizens or just outcasts? Aborigines are roped off in some of the picture halls, churches and other places. Various papers make crude jokes about us. We are slighted in all sorts of mean and petty ways. When I say that we are Australia's untouchables you must agree with me.

You will also agree with me that Australia would not and could not have been opened up successfully without my people's help and guidance of the white explorers. Hundreds of white men, women and children owe their very lives to Aborigine trackers and runners — tracking lost people. Quite a few airmen owe their lives to Aboriginals. I want you to remember that men of my race served in the Boer War, more so in the 1914–18 War and today hundreds of full-bloods, near full-bloods and half-castes are overseas with the AIF. More are joining each day. My own son is somewhere on the high seas serving with the Australian Navy. Many women of Aborigine blood are helping with war charities. Many are WRANS. We the Aborigines are proving to the world that we are not only helping to protect Australia but also the British Empire. New South Wales is the mother state and therefore should act as an inspiration to the rest of Australia. So we are asking for full citizenship and the status to be granted to us. We are asking that the 800 full-bloods in New South Wales be included in the claim — all those who are deprived of all federal social services to be granted, through the state, the old age pension and the maternity bonus until this injustice can be reformed by a federal law. We want an equal number of Aborigines as whites on the Welfare Board.

My friends, I'm asking for friendship. We Aborigines need help and encouragement, the same as you white people. We need to be cheered and encouraged to the ideals of citizenship. We ask help, education, encouragement from your white government. But the Aborigines Welfare gives us the stone of officialdom. Please remember, we don't want your pity, but practical help. This you can do by writing to the Hon. Chief Secretary, Mr Baddeley, MLA Parliament House, Sydney and ask that our claims be granted as soon as possible. Also that more white men who understand my people, such as the chairman, Mr Michael Sawtell, be appointed to the Board — not merely government officials. We expect more reforms from the new government. By doing this you will help to pay off the great debt that you, the white race, owe to my Aboriginal people. I would urge, may I beg you, to hand my Aboriginal people the democracy and the Christianity that you, the white nation of Australia, so proudly boast of. I challenge the white nation to make these boasts good. I'm asking your practical help for a new and better deal for my race. Remember we, the Aboriginal people, are the creditors. Do not let it be said of you that we have asked in vain. Will my appeal for practical humanity be in vain? I leave the answer to each and every one of you.

Measured against modern blacks' ideas of what justice for the Aboriginal race must entail, Pearl Gibbs' appeal was pretty moderate. There was no protest against the enormity of the theft of a continent. There was no compensation claim, no call for self-determination — the blacks were too down. Pearl's appeal was in terms of the preoccupations of the day — pensions, citizenship, a baby bonus, equal representation on the Board and so forth. The actual reforms asked for show the degree to which Aborigines were outcasts in their own country. They were not counted in anything. They were not considered in anything. Even small gains were monumental. One of the reasons why 'land rights' is not an issue in Pearl's talk is because many blacks in those days laboured under the illusion that 'Aboriginal Reserves' meant just that — land reserved to the blacks forever. Another generation was to disillusion them about this, as, all over New

South Wales, pieces of black reserves were sold or leased to land-hungry graziers. (Is it any wonder that the Country Party has always been such a strong political force against Aboriginal land rights? The alienation, too, has been considerably wider than many blacks realise. The recent 'land rights' concessions of the New South Wales government, announced as a pre-election stunt in 1972, listed Aboriginal land at Condobolin as seven acres. I remember when the reserve there was 300 acres. Similar situations prevail all over New South Wales.) In passing, too, notice that Pearl mentioned that there were 800 full-bloods in New South Wales in 1941. Also, says she, there were 194 full-blooded children. In 1941 she asked, 'What is going to happen to them?' Now it is possible to ask, 'What *did* happen to them?' Very rarely do you find a full-blood now, in any part of the state. At best there are only a handful left.

'Will my appeal for practical humanity be in vain?' asked Pearl Gibbs in 1941. Looking back, the answer, pretty well, was 'yes'. True, inchingly, excruciatingly, reforms were achieved. But none of them made any real dent in the ongoing situation and none of them were on a large enough scale, or bold enough to even begin to bring any healing to the people. It was not until May 1973 that Aboriginal patriot Pearl Gibbs, now seventy-two years of age and as conversant as ever with developments in Aboriginal affairs, tentatively said 'big things are happening'.

In 1941 blacks were calling for citizenship rights. The 1967 Referendum saw white Australia conferring that right. It gave the federal government power to override state legislation and take direct action on behalf of Aborigines. The fact that, five years later, the federal government had still not even begun to tackle the 'Aboriginal problem' and had, indeed, spent a lot of time and energy trying to deny, ignore or whitewash the realities of it shows how strong white racist resistance to black aspirations in the Liberal–Country Party coalition was.

Of the states, Queensland was and is the worst. Despite periodic amendments of the various Acts that regulate black lives in Queensland, blacks say that the spirit of white paternalism and black subjugation remains unchanged. True, as Senator Bonner has pointed out, many of the amendments made have been as recommended by the Aboriginal councillors on the reserves. But as other blacks are quick to point out, you don't get to be a councillor unless you are a good jacky who is totally under the manager's thumb in the first place. The following comments, made by Mick Miller, a school teacher living in Cairns and vice-president of FCAATSI (Federal Council for the Advancement of Aborigines and Torres Strait Islanders) are strongly reminiscent of Pearl Gibbs' complaints in New South Wales over thirty years earlier. Mick was speaking in September '72:

> I have in mind two missions that have been particularly badly treated, Weipa and Hopevale. At Weipa, the bauxite is mined by Comalco and there's sand mining at Cape Flattery. Weipa and this part of Cape Flattery belong to an Aboriginal reserve. Between the Presbyterian church and the state government and Comalco they came to some sort of an arrangement whereby Comalco could go in and take out the bauxite. The people at Weipa weren't even asked for their opinion.
>
> No mention was made of the people being given jobs, or any royalty being paid because it was their reserve. Nothing at all. They were just told to move. They had to move back from where this bauxite was located. The actual area the mission is on now is chopped right down to about 410 acres. Now it once consisted of over a million acres, that reserve at Weipa. They're pushed back, into a place called South Weipa and isolated from the rest of the community. There are a couple of thousand people in this mining town of Weipa, but the Aboriginal people have been shifted back a couple of miles. They can go into town, but they have to be out of there by a certain hour.
>
> Jobs were an issue there at one stage. Because it is on their reserve, we feel that the people should be given jobs, be trained, and given comparable wages. They mucked about with that for a while and then brought in a clause which they call a 'slow worker's' clause. Nearly all the

Aborigines working at Weipa are under it, which gives the boss there the right to pay them maybe $30–40 a week — less than half the ordinary average wage up there. This clause lets the company out. They just nominate how many fellows they want, without testing the working capacity of any of the Aboriginal fellows up there and, I know this for a fact, they are straightaway labelled 'slow workers'. There's no great benefit from Comalco at all. Last year [1971] Comalco made a gesture of handing over so many thousands of shares to the people of Weipa. But in reality those shares are controlled by the Department of Native Affairs for Queensland. So the people can't just benefit from them like you or I could. They are controlled by the Department of Native Affairs. They say when those people take the money out and how much is to be spent. And when.

Take 'The Act'. They amend it every so many years — the 1971 amendment is not law yet. Now this Act governs between 30,000–40,000 Aborigines in Queensland. Their lives are controlled on land set aside for their use and governed by a manager. Now he is the Almighty. He has to administer that Act. In practice he interprets it how he likes because who is there to challenge him? In a lot of cases blacks still can't travel without his permission, can't accept visitors into their homes — even relatives. The whole theme is paternalism. For example for years we've had blacks classed as 'assisted'. It doesn't mean that any assistance is given to you — it simply means that you are controlled by the Native Affairs Act. It's just a paternalistic term that they brought in which helped them to prove that the Aborigine needed helping because he is such a darn loafer, bludger, sponger that he needs someone to help him. The Department likes to give the impression that the Aborigine has to be assisted. Otherwise he'd just fall over in the gutter and that'd be the end of him. So that's how the term came in. He's being helped by the Department!

There aren't any industries on the reserves, unless you take Weipa and Hopevale. The other reserves have some timber milling, farming, dairying and market gardening, but it's only marginal. There is no industry of a scale big enough to serve another community. This has been knocked out of them years ago. They've been told that *they* 'need to be supplied' — it's an idea that has been ingrained into them ever since they were kids. They believe that they can't do these sort of things and the Department wouldn't allow it if they tried. They'd rather get supplies from the towns to supply the native community and just let the people there exist in their little jobs of boat-building or road-making or timber milling. The highest pay in one of those settlements would be between $36 and $40 a fortnight. I could show you wage sheets: 'Head stockmen' $30 per fortnight. Three offsiders $18 or $20 per fortnight. Out of that they have to pay their rent. Measuring their rent against their income, it is pretty high — they have to pay about $5–$8 per fortnight. That's a lot of money when you're only getting about $20–$36 and you've got children going to school.

Weipa is in the Gulf of Carpentaria. On the other side of the peninsula from Weipa, you're coming onto the Barrier Reef side. There is a reserve, or a settlement there called Hopevale. That is the other example I was going to give you. It's a pretty big area — there's about a quarter of a million acres there I think and it stretches right down to the sea. Where it touches the sea, there are these great big sand dunes and they've got all these minerals in the sands. One of the mining companies have been mining there for about six years or more. To begin with they did employ Hopevale Aborigines. But the latest count which I got about three weeks ago from a fellow from Lockhart, another settlement there, said that there'd be no more than seven Aborigines working on the mineral sands there now. And this would be the time they'd be expected to be taking on more workers because they've just signed a couple of contracts with Japan for something like 50,000 tons of rutile. Places like Weipa, Cape Flattery, Hopevale are always advertising for labour and yet they've got a labour pool right close at hand and they won't even use it. The Aborigines, given training, would give good work if they knew they were getting good money. There isn't any doubt about that.

The people of Hopevale do not receive one measley cent from the mining. Nothing at all, even though it's their reserve land being mined. They've had a go at protesting to the authorities. They were just told that a royalty wouldn't be paid. Because they didn't have a deed to the land, the land wasn't theirs in reality. It was just mission land, but it wasn't the Aborigines' land. The Lutheran mission controls the whole of that area. The mining companies would've had to deal with the mission. The missions, the state government and the companies — it's them all the time. The mission itself doesn't get any royalty either. But it is interesting that the church that controls this mission is the one that Premier Bjelke-Petersen goes to. The mission authorities made no attempts to stop the mining or intervene to get the Hopevale people any sort of a deal.

Another thing we're concerned about is the legislation dealing with police handling of Aborigines. It is so easy to arrest an Aboriginal and have him charged. We're also trying to get rid of the passbook system. The passbook is their bank book. A lot of their money — they don't get their full wages, they get part of their wages and the rest is put into a trust fund — goes into government hands. We're trying to do away with that. We've brought up examples of misappropriation of funds by the 'protectors' who are supposed to be looking after these Aborigines. Cases of fellers swiping $5000! They're caught and sent to jail, but not for a very long term. And this goes on all the time. We've taken complaints about these sorts

> of things — complaints about police bashings, arrest, misappropriation of funds, etc. And of course we're trying to do away with the Act. We're bringing up examples all the time of how unjust and cruel it is.

The Queensland state secretary's report at the sixteenth annual conference of FCAATSI, held in Brisbane in April '73 stated that a new Aborigines Act and a new Torres Strait Islanders Act and regulations had been proclaimed.

> But in spite of all this, Aborigines and Islanders are still mostly in the same position they've always been. People still have to submit to the same old indignity of procuring a 'pass' or a permit before they can go to a mission or settlement to visit their relatives or friends. Of course the permits are granted by the Aboriginal councils. But only three councillors out of five are elected and the white manager makes sure the people who are elected are the manager's choice.

FCAATSI President Joe McGinness, at the same conference, said that the legislation was:

> a serious handicap to our people's struggle for equality. Those who exercise the authority and control through this special legislation like to argue that this is not the case. However no country in the world, other than South Africa, has similar suppressive legislation that forces its indigenous population into unnecessary hardships and because of this we should have no hesitancy in supporting the call that the federal government make use of its constitutional powers gained through the 1967 Referendum to take over the responsibility of Aboriginal affairs from all states.

Under Gorton there had been some chance of this occurring, although on July 12, 1968 in an address to the conference of

Commonwealth and state ministers responsible for Aboriginal affairs he said:

> In fact, of course, the powers of the Commonwealth are paramount in the sense that in any conflict of law its law will prevail. But there is no such conflict at present and I have every confidence that none will arise.

Under McMahon there was no chance of federal intervention. At the conference of ministers for Aboriginal affairs at Cairns on April 23, 1971 he said:

> I am happy to inform Ministers that discussions with the states, following the agreement reached at this conference a year ago to examine remaining legislation which appears to discriminate against Aborigines, have proceeded amicably and promise well for a successful outcome. Thereafter it will be our task, with, I believe, the support of the great mass of Australian people, to move towards the complete enjoyment of normal civil liberties by Aborigines generally.

The blacks had heard it all before. Nothing had changed. Nor would it, while the Liberal–Country Party coalition governed.

The degree to which the prevailing winds *had* changed by 1973 was apparent in early March when Labor Minister for Aboriginal Affairs, Gordon Bryant, speaking at Charters Towers said, regarding the Queensland Acts:

> There is no reason why these laws, with their widespread infringements of fundamental human rights, should continue in 1973. Thousands of Queensland Aborigines and Islanders under the Acts have their property managed by a 'protector' of the State Department of Aboriginal and Island Affairs. Often in small towns, this person, who decides how much the Aboriginal and Island people should have of their own wages, is the local policeman.

> How many people in the rest of the community would put up with a system where they were reduced to pleading with a policeman for a few dollars of their own money? What particularly disturbs me is that mothers are not even receiving their endowment payments without this interference. The whole principle of child endowment is that it should go to the mother. Only in Queensland have you got the government standing between the people and their just rights. It must be the most humiliating social service procedure left in Australia. I will be discussing ways of stopping the interference with wages and social services with the Minister for Labour, Mr Clyde Cameron, the Minister for Social Security, Mr Bill Hayden, and the Treasurer, Mr Frank Crean, who has the jurisdiction to prevent the Commonwealth Bank being used as an agent of the Queensland government in this area.

The failure of the Australian government and public to act, in McMahon's words, to 'end racial discrimination in our midst and to deal with Aboriginal Australians with respect, justice, humanity and compassion' led directly to the formation of the Black Panther movement in Queensland. Various Queensland blacks began exhorting the Aboriginal people to break the usurpers' chains and urged people to strike for human dignity and freedom. They also called on Aborigines to defend themselves in whatever manner necessary to stop violence against them.

But the real focus of black affairs was Redfern (Sydney) and soon, Canberra. Dr Coombs had warned in the *Australian Journal of Education* in October, 1971:

> After 170 odd years of decline the Aboriginal population is now rising rapidly and a failure to solve the educational and other problems of their place in our society could mean that the fond illusion many of us hold of Australia as homogenous and free of 'race' problems could be dissipated in violence and hatred.

In Sydney, thanks to white professional help, the blacks had set up the badly needed Aboriginal Legal Service (Paul Coe said he was sick of being belted up by coppers), the Aboriginal Medical Service and later, the Aboriginal Breakfast Programme, the Moratorium for Black Rights Committee and the Black Caucus. Such organisations tackled the problems of black inequality before the law, black health, protest and so forth and were set up by black youngsters because they believed that the leadership of Aboriginal affairs had long passed from token organisations such as the New South Wales branch of FCAATSI or the Foundation for Aboriginal Affairs. Redfern, not city centre, was the centre of black affairs.

On Australia Day, January 26, 1972, Prime Minister McMahon brought out his land denial policy for Aborigines. Blacks were not, in principle, to be given land rights because this implicitly threatened the 'security of tenure' of white landowners. However, the government had decided to grant special purpose leases to continuing Aboriginal groups and communities. These leases would only be granted if the government felt that the blacks had demonstrated adequate 'economic or social' use for them. Of course there would still be none of that 'security of tenure' so dear to white Australians' hearts. Minister for the Environment, Aborigines and the Arts, Peter Howson — who was described by columnist Phillip Adams as a 'pain in the Arts' — suggested that the new swindle represented 'an imaginative attempt to adapt Australian forms to fit in with Aboriginal ideas in relation to land'. Such was the type of sophistry with which Aborigines were once again shielded from getting some of the nitty-gritty. Howson has since, thankfully, not only ceased to be a minister but lost his seat in the December [1972] elections.

The Australia Day statement, as it happened, came at a time when blacks had arrived at a particularly depressing point of morale. In 1967 they had hoped that with the granting of citizenship rights and federal power to override state legislation, conditions would improve for Aborigines and land rights would be a possibility. Instead of this, blacks witnessed the official bullying of the Gurindji tribe, which was attempting to claim

500 square miles of country at Wattie Creek, Northern Territory. Then came the decision in the *Gove Land Rights* case which found against the Yirrkala tribe's land claim on the Gove Peninsula. The release of official figures showing that black infants were dying at between ten and seventeen times the rate for white babies in various parts of the country, was enough to depress blacks even further.

That was why the Aboriginal Embassy came into being. After it had been standing on the lawns before Parliament House, Canberra for several months, Country Party minister Ralph Hunt published a booklet entitled 'Aboriginal Land Rights and the Northern Territory'. It was a succinct outline of how the anti-black landed interests of this country think. Stated Hunt:

> European Australians who have sweated to carve a nation out of a desolate continent have a legitimate stake in this country and security of title of land is paramount in an orderly society. The claim for $6 billion compensation for dispossession of land in the past, which has been made by some groups of Aboriginals inspired by radical groups, flows quite naturally from the argument that Aborigines anywhere in Australia have a moral, if not a legal right to land based on ancestral association with that land.

Aborigines, of course, do not deny that whites have carved out a stake in Australia. As one rather ruefully, tongue in cheek, stated: 'I guess we have to face the fact that the gubbah is here to stay.' All that blacks are asking is for material recognition of the fact that *their* 30,000 years of prior occupancy counts for something too. The material recognition must be in terms of land and compensation. But in Hunt's view, the Aborigine was obviously not capable of making such a claim. Therefore it must have been 'inspired by radical groups' out to foment trouble for the government. Accordingly the booklet warned that 'unfortunately there are indications that the 144,000 Aborigines will be used as a political football this year'. It did go on to admit that 'since the European settlement, the Australian Aborigines have suffered one injustice after another, and they have gone from one disability to another'. Nevertheless it was obvious that the Embassy's call for land rights was not a true Aboriginal people's movement but was dominated by left wing or communist elements.

Here are the facts of the matter. Just before the McMahon statement, when word had already got through that it would be another land denial, I called together a number of young Aboriginal militants, Michael Anderson, Gary Williams, Tony Coorey, Billy Craigie and Gary Foley and discussed with them the need for a permanent peaceful land rights demonstration outside Parliament House in Canberra. Excluding Gary Foley, who suddenly found that he had 'other important business elsewhere' these blacks agreed to go to Canberra as soon as sufficient funds were available. As I had planned for concurrent demos outside the parliament house in each state, Gary Williams stayed in Sydney to try to organise one in New South Wales, while telegrams were sent to Jack Davis in Western Australia, Pastor Doug Brady in Queensland as well as other leaders in other states. (It is a matter of history that the idea of concurrent demonstrations did not come off.) Next problem was how to get the money for Canberra. I had not long been out of jail and had no union contacts whatsoever, so I accompanied Michael Anderson to the Waterside Workers Union offices where Mr Fitzgibbon sent out a terse message to Anderson that he was 'too busy' to see him. It was obviously time to move to the left, so next I rang Alex Robertson and Dennis Freney at the *Tribune* and told them of the need for a Canberra demo. We needed a car and funds to get the initial group to Canberra. Would they help? They agreed without any conditions or demurral whatsoever and supplied us with a car and a cheque for $70 which I cashed through my personal account and gave to Michael Anderson.

From its inception to its demise, the Aboriginal Embassy was a totally Aboriginal thing. Besides treating us with ordinary courtesy at its inception and providing the car and funds to kick it off, the Communists had no influence over it nor did they exercise any control. Thank Christ for Commos! They know that Aborigines don't give a damn for their dogma, any more than they do for the dogmas of the bible bashers, but they are nevertheless willing to give practical aid to blacks more often, more reliably and unconditionally than other groups. If that is 'manipulation', more power to it.

After this impetus, my connection with the Embassy ceased and it became the vehicle for young radical protest. It certainly achieved the purpose for which it was intended. Although I regret that the land claim put out by the Embassy was not a little more realistic, the way all of black Australia responded to that little tent in Canberra and the idea of land rights shows the unanimity of black thinking as to ultimate ends. I could never, myself, go to Canberra at any time while the Embassy was standing. Parole regulations keep me confined to the anachronistic Eastern Lands Division of New South Wales. Each movement outside this area must be sanctioned by the state governor and applied for a fortnight in advance. If I step outside this area without official permission, I am liable to be returned to a life sentence. This fact I never could get into the heads of the young radicals who felt that I did not have the guts to follow up the chain of events that I had started. Of course, for me to go to Canberra without permission would have been a fruitless exercise in defiance. I did, at the time, make the required formal application to go to Canberra but permission was refused by the New South Wales parole authorities. Of course there was 'legitimate' reason for needing to go to Canberra as well — a fact that Mr Barry Dexter, Director of the then Office of Aboriginal Affairs confirmed. But the New South Wales authorities would not let me anywhere near Canberra at any time that the Embassy was standing.

The Embassy started off as a land rights demonstration. But as Paul Coe has said since:

> Tony Coorey got the idea of calling the tent the 'Aboriginal Embassy'. It started off as a joke, but turned out to be perhaps one of the most brilliant symbolic forms of protest that this country had ever seen. The reason why the Embassy became such a powerful thing was because in many ways it typified the history of this country: the

> invasion, colonisation, the arrogance of the white man, imposing his values and his culture on other people.

And Bobbi Sykes:

> The Embassy symbolised that blacks had been pushed as far back as blacks are going to be pushed. That from now on, they are going forward again. Despite people fighting and struggling right across the country, spasmodically, individually, in isolation, the first *national* announcement that the pushing back was going to stop was the Embassy. Despite FCAATSI and that stuff. The Embassy was a *black* affair; it wasn't blacks being guided by whites. And I was determined to keep it so. First and foremost it symbolised the land rights struggle. But beyond that it said to white Australia, 'You've kicked us down for the last time.' In all areas. In education, in health, in police victimisation, in locking people up en masse — in all these things. It said that blacks were now going to get up and fight back on any or all these issues.

The details about the removal of the Embassy, the police violence and its aftermath are all reasonably familiar to Australians. As far as the cops were concerned, they had to get a tent off the lawns. The blacks, on the other hand, weren't just fighting for a tent — they were fighting for the whole of Australia, for the land, the dying babies, the misery.

Of course that 'ragged little symbol of hope' as Bobbi called it, had become too much of an embarrassment for the government to tolerate any longer. Said Coe:

> It got to the stage where they couldn't tolerate it any longer because we were getting international publicity. We were getting a big exposé of the situation of Aboriginal people in Australia and the federal government was being criticised in the world press — *The New York Times*, the London *Times*, Japanese newspapers, *TASS* Soviet newsagency

and even *The Peking Daily* ran stories. When it got to this level they decided they'd had enough of this. They might've thought that if it was allowed to go on, it might get to the stage where some of their exports could've been jeopardised by embargoes being placed against Australia. I personally believe this. I think they saw all sorts of situations where Australia would be treated like Rhodesia — with economic blockades, United Nations imposed. That would've been the outcome of the Embassy if it had stayed there much longer.

3

Australian Racism

PADDY

I'm black Paddy. I pick grapes
An' I trap rabbits
One extreme to the other
Sweet juices on my hands one week
Stinkin' rabbits guts the next
I don't eat 'flash' most of the time
Sometimes chops, sometimes hash
Mostly sugar/flour/tea, goannas that I seek
Moolingmah 'n gullingah (sheep guts)
An' other butchers trash
It does me. I'm a trapper — but I'm FREE
Know what it's like, boy?
It's like the sweet spring breeze singin' in the tree
The clean face of the moon on a winter's night
The powerful pound of the sea.
No man calls me 'Jacky'
No man counts weekly pennies into my hand
No man cheats me or patronizes me
No man calls me 'darky' or 'boy'
No man calls me anything but 'Sir' and 'Mr Patrick'
It's great to be free, worthwhile to be free

Even if you have to trap rabbits and eat sheep guts —
Eat well of it — not for the hell of it
Eat sheep guts — and fight to be FREE!!!

Individuals raising their voice in protest against the inequities under which Aborigines labour are not a new development in Aboriginal affairs. There was, however, as late as the 'sixties, no 'Aboriginal movement' as such to back them. As Chicka Dixon recalls:

> Looking back on the movement, from the time we went on the 1963 Freedom Rides to Moree and Walgett, things have changed tremendously. In those days you could only get two blacks involved — me and Charlie Perkins — with a lot of white students on a bus. Today, when you ask blacks to move on a certain issue, you can get a heap of them. But not then. Even up until '68 when we tried to march 'em down George St to support the Gurindjis, you could count the blacks on your fingers, or, at the most fifteen or twenty. Now we can muster 600 or more, so the pendulum has swung. We have just started to move. The things we were trying to crack in those days are exactly what we are up against today. What we were trying to do was to go into those racist towns and establish beyond a shadow of a doubt that discrimination and prejudice did exist. That was the idea of blowing those towns up. Because white people are so complacent. Apathy and complacency — even blokes I work with on the waterfront, blokes who are pretty militant, didn't believe that some of the things we were saying were really true. We wanted to show Australia what really existed in these outback towns. For example, in those days, in Moree. Black kids weren't free to go in the swimming baths. Blacks couldn't go where they chose in the picture show. At Walgett they weren't allowed to drink out of the glasses in a local milk bar. Young girls weren't allowed to try on dresses in a frock shop there. And, of course, there was the pub discrimination. These were

> the things that we were trying to pick up, the grassroots discrimination that we were trying to bring out into the open. This is what we were trying to draw attention to with the Embassy. You've got to link up all the things together — bad housing, land rights, infant mortality, bad education facilities, all the things we've bashed at for years while nothing was done. Yet, when blacks stood up on their feet, then things started moving. And I believe that we've only scratched the surface.

The need for something resembling a 'black movement' in an organised sense became more apparent to Aboriginals in the 'sixties and 'seventies and was expressed in the formation of the short-lived National Tribal Council which foundered on administrative weaknesses, personal rivalries and faction fighting. The need for unity was recognised, but not met. Other black initiatives, however, were more successful. Says Charles Perkins:

> Every effort in Aboriginal affairs has played its part. The Freedom Rides were designed to focus attention on the shocking conditions in New South Wales country towns. These conditions are pretty well the same still. The only difference is that now people are taking notice. Attempts to change things are under way. That was the idea — to jar people to the fact that people were suffering, that something had to be done, that things didn't have to go on just as they were. The Freedom Rides were only a stage in this. They didn't answer all problems and weren't the only thing of consequence that has happened. Like the Embassy, the Rides made their contribution to the whole. The 1967 Referendum 'yes' vote was brought about by all of these pressures — Freedom Rides, people speaking, the active organisations, individuals. All these added up to an unprecendented 'yes' vote. But after that, it was a dismal failure because the Commonwealth government — the Liberal–Country Party coalition — was a disaster for

> Aborigines. It just didn't want to implement the spirit of the Referendum. This brought about a great frustration in Aboriginal affairs after the Referendum. The frustration was to find its expression in a new mood amongst blacks in the 'seventies, a mood which was quickly to be labelled by the newspapers as 'black power' but which is more accurately set under the general label of 'assertion of black dignity'.

Australia, despite a common Aboriginal jibe, is not a down-under South Africa, however much it may have gone in for segregation in its past history. With the exception of Queensland, labelled as Australia's 'deep north', Australian racism is not so institutionalised, so organised as South Africa's. This is the general situation even though examples contradicting this view are not hard to find in our recent history and even up to today. Of course, the only reason why Australian racism is not like that in South Africa is because here blacks are not numerous enough and have therefore not been perceived as enough of a threat to warrant it. Where 'apartheid' conditions prevail, they have been instituted to suit white convenience rather than fear. Whites' convenience, apathy, 'I'm alright Jack' and a feeling of 'let the government do it' have for many years been the reaction of white Australians to revelations of black suffering in this country. As Gerry Bostock put it:

> The voting public don't give a damn about the Aboriginal question. They don't give a damn about black babies dying. Don't even give a damn about their own old people and pensioners dying. They're only worried about their consumption of alcohol at the pub, talk of sex, and who's going to win the Melbourne Cup. Sport, sex and piss — that's all they care about.

Gerry Bostock, incidentally, is an Aboriginal ex-serviceman who resigned from his job as a clerk in the Mines Department in Sydney when the police forcibly pulled down the Aboriginal

Embassy last year [1972]. He began to ask himself questions like 'why did I spend nine years fighting for so-called Australian freedom when other Aborigines like me can't get even the most basic freedoms?' He didn't like the obvious answers to such questions and felt compelled to quit his job in protest.

All human beings discriminate between various levels of human behaviour and categorise them as something to which they aspire or as something which they condemn. By this process personal standards are formed. But racist discrimination tends to ascribe to a whole group the patterns of behaviour that can be observed amongst the lowest individuals within that group. In short, it ceases to discriminate, and becomes mere prejudice. Most white Australians are prejudiced in some way, although very few seem to be aware of it. The mass media, in my experience, consistently censors out references to white racism. After all, how can something exist if you steadfastly refuse to admit to its possibility?

White Australian racism is something that is uniquely Australian, different in expression from the sex-obsessed racism of the United States or the garrison-fear racism of South Africa. (That is not to say that the sexual element isn't there. Sexual exploitation and abuse of the Aboriginal woman is constant. But Australians have not become obsessed about the Aboriginal male in the way that the southern USA is obsessed with male Negro sexuality. The symbolic castration murders are not a feature here as they are in the 'deep south'.) Yes, the expression is different, but its practical results on the psychology of blacks in this country is quite as devastating as anything seen in those countries. Psychologically, the Australian Aboriginal is right down.

If you don't believe it, go look in any country town at blacks walking along the streets. Note the sidelong, averted gaze, the exaggerated attempts at dignity, the overdone, affected bravado of Aborigines who know they are not accepted, who know they are outcasts and misfits in their own country. That is why the Aborigines who have come through the experience of being black in a white country with relatively little crippling, the

Aborigines who have managed to retain real personal dignity, are so strong on the racist theme. Every black knows what it is like. Take Bobbi Sykes' experiences:

> I was born in Townsville and educated until I was fourteen. At the time there was what amounted to a non-verbal policy not to educate blacks any further. I was told in no uncertain terms that I was not to come to school any more. That was it. So, I went to work. For a while with a newsagent. Nursed for a year. Worked in a factory. Scrubbed floors. Waited on tables. Did the washing up at the Mater Hospital in Brisbane. My journalism sort of ran parallel with all this and was an intermittent thing. I was writing, when I was about twelve, for children's magazines. Then I gave that away as having been successful. And then I didn't write anything for years. I wrote again when I was twenty, about things that were happening — things like my son's expulsion from kindergarten on racist grounds — things like that. Things that were happening to me personally, at the time, the time that I was moving around with my young son. It was fairly difficult for me to be involved with anything. It was a case of just getting enough money to stay alive.
>
> No one thing brought me into Aboriginal affairs. As I recall, my earliest experience of racism was when I was at school. It was virtually an all-white school except for myself and my sisters. There weren't any other blacks around to stick up with me if we ever got called names. So, being the oldest, I was the defender of myself and my sisters. I assure you there were plenty of racists at that school — it was an area where the black round-ups took place less than seventy years before ... From those days, I have always been a defender of myself and whoever is around me. I fought my way through school, through racist victimisation by school people — I could hardly call them companions — and then I left school. Next, I attempted to battle within my own limits against the Establishment, by

> forcing myself into jobs where 'no blacks need apply' or by forcing myself into places where they didn't serve blacks. I encouraged my sisters to do the same. Whenever we got turfed out of places, which often did happen, we'd write to the newspapers about it or we would get some friends and all go down to the place concerned. Don't forget that I'm talking here about sixteen year olds — long before this sort of stand was popular — and in Townsville, where this sort of thing is not even done today. Well, we'd go down to the milk bar whatever and take them on. So I don't think that I consciously moved into Aboriginal politics. I feel that I'd always been a civil rights fighter.

In Bobbi's case her early experiences of racism had her up and fighting. The majority retreat. A strong factor in this retreat is the Aboriginals' continuing fear of white violence. Even in New South Wales there are plenty of reserve blacks left who can remember the last occasion when armed whites rode into their camp for a shoot-up while local police turned a blind eye. And the fear of more subtle reprisals is an ever present one amongst blacks.

Of course, as Bobbi Sykes has pointed out, it is really not valid to speak of 'Australian racism' as though it means the same thing all through the nation. In fact it varies from state to state, from area to area and according to whatever ruling political ideology prevails. Bobbi Sykes made this point while commenting on her recent overseas trip to publicise the Aboriginal situation in this country:

> I had more television exposure in England in three months than most people would get in a lifetime. I did radio broadcasts for Radio Europe, Radio Asia and Radio Africa. I also did broadcasts in Switzerland that were translated into every European language. They were mainly short analyses of prevailing conditions. What I was trying to do was to get people to relate to Australia, not as a nation, but state by state. Because nobody ever says 'How's things in

Africa?' People say that there's a revolution going on in South Africa, and there's revolutionary processes at work in Angola and Mozambique and there's an uprising in Ghana. State by state, because they're all different. But in Australia, people even *in* Australia tend to think about the country as a whole when they think about blacks. Instead of the situation being different, state by state, which it *is*. All the blacks in Australia do not live under South Africa-like conditions. But the blacks in Queensland definitely do. They've got dual legislation, reserves, Bjelke-Petersen, South African-style reserve managers ... Queensland is a little South Africa, with a similar mentality. But you can't say that is so in Victoria. And you can't even say it for the Northern Territory. The reasons why things are as they are in the Northern Territory is for distinctly different reasons than those existing in Queensland. In Queensland the people are being forcibly, systematically oppressed. For economic motives, for power motives and things like this. Whereas in the Northern Territory they're still hoping that the blacks are going to die out. They've given that one up in Queensland but in the Northern Territory they still feel that if they just wait long enough, the blacks *will* all die. At least I got the impression that that was what they felt before December '72. I don't know what they are thinking now we have a new government. Everything pointed to them thinking that the blacks would die if they were patient. The health services were never improved, there was no attempt to teach English to the tribes as a second language and so on. None of it was set up because it was felt that if you just leave them alone and don't set up any of these programmes, eventually the blacks will go away.

So it is not only a good idea for people overseas to think of Australia state by state, but for Australians to do so too. It's up to the blacks in Victoria, who have the best living standards of blacks in Australia, to help their less fortunate brothers. I'm not saying that Victorian blacks

> are as well off as whites, or even that they are very well off at all, but they're certainly a lot better off than the Alice Springs people or the Queensland people. So therefore it becomes the problem of the Victorian people to do something on behalf of the Queensland people — if they are going to support national black liberation throughout Australia.

The stirrings for black justice that we have witnessed so far this century have already met an opposing force — generally called 'white backlash'. A fair number of Australians tend to begrudge any concerted efforts to raise the living standards of Aborigines. The protestant ethic dies hard — Australians do tend to believe that if the black man will strive as they strove, that he, too, can achieve the same status as they have achieved. To the stars through industry and application. Yet they know that in reality it isn't quite that simple. So, a member of a white backlash group in the Northern Territory, June Tapp, interviewed on the ABC television programme *With Gerald Stone* on April 15 this year asked: 'Well, why not sit down under a tree all day? Why go to school? I mean, really, if they're happy doing that ... of course I think that since the grog's come in and because their whole tribal structure has gone they're not really happy.' No, they're not. That is the basic underlying fact that has set so many white-inspired schemes for black 'betterment' or 'advancement' to nought. That is the basic fact that has made a mockery of all the European-inspired protection programmes, welfare programmes, assimilation programmes and God knows what that our people have endured for generations now. To be *unhappy and ill-adjusted* is the core thing, the root thing. Added to this is the fact that those who advocate the 'get up and go' ethic for blacks disregard such things as unfair discrimination against blacks in employment (the last to be hired; first to be fired), the fact that blacks generally only get the lousiest jobs and then usually on a non-permanent basis. They totally lack appreciation, too, of the fact that most Aborigines *are* victims of a complex chain of social and historical circumstances that have made them cripples in the truest sense of the word, even though they may not literally be confined to wheelchairs.

Said our wonderfully quotable 'Nugget' Coombs in his address to the conference of the Australian College of Education in Canberra in May 1970:

> It is certain that the health of Aboriginal children falls far short of acceptable standards and of that of white Australian children. Research in Aboriginal communities of the centre and north, among the fringe-dwellers of country towns, and among the part-Aborigines of the cities reveals widespread malnutrition, beginning often in the immediate post-weaning period and in many cases imposing a permanent handicap in physical and mental development. Aboriginal children suffer much more than is normal for our society from gastro-enteritis, from otitus media, from respiratory infections, from glaucoma and other eye troubles to a degree which frequently leaves them lethargic and unresponsive to normal stimuli.

Anyone who moves about amongst Aboriginal groups will be immediately struck by the low standard of health that prevails. To almost perenially have something wrong is accepted as a natural part of life by many of our people. How can it be otherwise? On the one hand there has been, to a greater or lesser extent, depending on the area, imperfect nutrition over succeeding generations. This cannot but have its impact on the bodies and constitutions of today's Aborigines. On the other hand, the adverse emotional/psychological climate that prevails on the reserves also does its damage — often a greater damage, even, than the history of poor nutrition. As Dr Coombs also pointed out in the same address:

> Generally Aboriginal children come from a background of poverty. The material consequences of this are serious enough, but the lack of intellectual stimulus may be educationally even more damaging. There is good reason

> to believe that, in the development of language and intellectual concepts upon which future attainment will be built, the pre-schools are critical; that, in respect of these elements, learning capacity is fixed in time and that stunting of the learning process during that time is irretrievable and cannot be compensated for by later attempts at enrichment. Work by Dr B. Nurcombe in Bourke, New South Wales has shown that by the time Aboriginal children get to school, they are, in terms of intellectual stimulation, already eighteen months to two years behind standard white performance. It is probable that the gap will widen rather than narrow.

Every Aboriginal who has lived on any of the reserves knows this. Every such Aboriginal, when asked, repeats over and over again that the only way that an answer can come is when white Australia gives blacks a just land base and the financial means to allow communities to begin to help themselves. 'Being done to' by Europeans has never worked and will never work. Blacks must *themselves* seek to strip off the crippling burdens of apathy, ignorance and soul loss that have plagued them for so long. And how can there be healing when Aboriginal communities continue to feel that the white man has not acknowledged that wrong was done? Until Australia gives material and financial recognition of the fact that that wrong was done, there is little chance of any alteration. While this nation does not recognise and make substantial compensation and land restoration gestures to Aborigines, including the part-Aborigines of the south, then in the minds of all blacks, the Australian claim to nationhood continues to rest on injustice and hypocrisy.

Very few whites, even at university level, know very much about the black experience in this country. They don't realise that racism is a daily experience for most blacks, in shops, in jobs, in the street. A black woman has a job cleaning rooms in a motel. She has worked there several years and has given satisfaction during that time. The motel changes hands and she is given notice to quit. The new boss feels that a black face on the premises might cost him business. So, out she goes. You can see Aborigines standing patiently awaiting their turn in a shop. Everybody around them is served, including those out of turn. Only when the shop is empty will the shop assistant deign to serve the black person. On the street there are the eyes, staring at black skin. There are the taunts, the deliberate rudeness, the obstruction. Don't tell me that it can't be so. It is. Ask any Aboriginal person. Yet people are amazed to hear that this is a racist country because after all, 'I'm not a racist'. Maybe, but many are and racist discrimination is constantly being experienced by blacks.

As union organiser Harry Anderson of the Newcastle branch of the Miscellaneous Workers' Union said, speaking about racism in the trade union movement,

> Even the committed ones, the left wing, see the problem in terms of 'doing something for them' rather than in terms of understanding what racism, including their own, is all about in the first place. None of them understand the nature of racism, which is the acceptance of someone as being on a lower level than oneself. This is the crucial issue.

Bob and Kaye Bellear are a couple who spend a considerable part of their lives battling against racism and the things it has wrought. Bob is black. His wife, Kaye, is white. Recently, in their flat in Kogarah they told me some of it.

> On November 14 last year, on a Friday night, Kaye and I were at the Empress Hotel in Redfern. The police were doing their usual round-up. There was this guy from north Queensland there. I told him to go home, told him that he'd probably get picked up because he was very black. Anyway, he didn't and he got pinched. The cops were dragging him down to the wagon and Kaye followed them and asked what he was being arrested for. They told her to piss off. They kept on hammering him and Kaye said that there was no need for it because he wasn't resisting or

fighting or anything. So she was told to piss off again. She kept protesting and after they told her for the third time to piss off she said, 'You've got to be a derelict to be a copper.' She was immediately arrested because one of the cops found that *most* offensive. They took her to Redfern police station to be charged.

*

While I was waiting to be charged, Bob came in after me and they told him to get out. That's when the business started about my wedding ring. The cops, four of them, took my wedding ring off. They nearly tore my hand off doing it. They tore my wedding ring off and threw it. This is the symbol that they just can't stand! A white woman has just cast them all aside and doesn't want anything to do with bloody gubs. It just kicks them that you're married to a black! Anyway, I was still waiting to be charged and this sergeant sidled up to me and said 'What's wrong with you, anyway, Kaye? Do you like being fucked by blacks?' So I called him a racist shit — and got another charge. So I've got to appear on March 20 on these two charges. I'm not going to deny that I said any of these things. But I will put it that 'You've got to be a derelict to be a copper' can't be unseemly when they were acting like derelicts. You know, derelicts in the strict sense of the word — outside the norms of human behaviour. And bashing someone who is drunk must be outside these norms. And asking me whether I like being fucked by blacks! Well, 'racist shit' is a perfect reply to something like that. So, where did I break the law by saying either of these things? But knowing that ——'ll be on the bench, we haven't got a show of beating it, I don't think. [She didn't. A $120 fine was duly imposed, but it was paid by a group of sympathetic professors!]

We also got arrested on New Year's Eve. Along with Bob English, one of the priests at the Redfern Rectory. It was the anti-Vietnam bombing meeting outside the Town Hall. Then about 500 of us marched up William St. The cops didn't come near us. Then about a hundred yards from the fountain they mowed in on bikes and Minis and things, and started running us down and running people onto the footpath. The next thing, I just got plucked. I was walking down the road, looking for Bob when I got grabbed. I was dragged over and the copper was giving me a bit of a thumping on the way over to the wagon. Then he handed me to another bloke. He kept up the thumping, so I lay on the ground. While I was laying on the ground, he just put the boot into my skull. The next thing I felt this great bloody weight coming through. Cops were going everywhere. That was Bob [Bellear]. Anyway he got charged with assault police and I got charged with unseemly words. Eventually they took us up to Darlinghurst. Took them ages to put us through the books; and all the insults you get, you know, like, 'Oh, don't worry about her, she's only married to a fuckin' boong', and, 'Don't worry Kaye, blackfellers aren't that bad. Every white man should have one.' All the usual things that they go on with all the time. Anyway, there were three or four other women arrested with me. There are no facilities for women down at Darlinghurst so we were taken down to Central. After about half an hour in the cells there I started to vomit. I was frightened that I might have concussion from the kicking I'd had. I had blurred vision and so on. After I'd demonstrated that I wasn't putting it on by vomiting three or four more times they finally decided to get me a doctor. An hour later, nobody had come and I still hadn't been taken to the hospital. So one of the Aboriginal girls in the cell with me — she's as funny as a circus — picked up one of the bed-boards and began banging it against the wall. Matron came up. 'What are you screamin' about?' And she said, 'If she was white you'd have her to a doctor straightaway. But just 'cause she's bloody black you won't

> take her to the hospital!' I don't know if that had any effect, but within five minutes they had two policemen and two policewomen to take me to the hospital. A big guard, you know. Yet I'd been charged with unseemly words! On the way up to the hospital, I started vomiting in the police car. I'd asked the copper to stop and he'd said 'You fuckin' vomit in this car and you'll fuckin' eat it!' So I thought, 'Damn you jack,' and I did, vomit, I mean. When I got to the hospital the doctor took me in and they followed me in too. I said to the doctor 'Look, I'm not going to be examined in front of them.' He agreed. One of the policewomen said 'She's our prisoner.' The doctor said 'Yes, and she's *my* patient. Get out.' So eventually I was released on $100 bail. The doctor had wanted to keep me in, but I was so distressed by the whole thing that I just wanted to come home. I've since taken out summonses against two cops for assault. Oh hell, it's just one continual process of fighting …

In a way, Bob and Kaye Bellear do ask for some of the trouble they get into but as Kaye explained:

> We're always on some new charge because I'm white and Bob's black and it's an affront to white society to be married to a black man. I mean it's not so bad if it's a black woman married to a white man. That's a step up. And society can sort of accept this, because they're welcoming this poor deprived woman into their bosom! I think it's because I insist, *insist* on being called Mrs Bellear and won't answer to anything else. I get some pretty rotten names but I just won't answer to them. I'm Mrs Bellear, and that's it. And they *don't* like it! But the main thing is the situation that I'm in. I go up to the police station at least three times a week, demanding to know why people have been arrested. I go in demanding to see people in those cells — people whom I think are going into the DTs. I demand to be allowed to go in to give them injections.

So I put myself into a situation where the police feel that their authority is being questioned all the time.

I must admit that I do play on it though. If Bob and I are pinched together I do walk up to him and put my arms around him and kiss him. In front of fifty cops. I know it upsets them. It really gets into their guts. But why not, man? Why not get into their guts?

4

The Election of Hope

The 1972 federal elections were of unprecedented interest to many southern Aboriginals who for generations had regarded elections as irrelevant to their lives. The year 1972 had seen the Liberal–Country Party government's land denial and the black response — the Aboriginal Embassy for land rights. The policy of the Labor Party was immeasurably more enlightened than that of the government and individuals within the Labor movement, particularly Senator Jim Keeffe, had repeatedly shown their sympathy with the tent Embassy. The twenty-ninth Federal Conference of the ALP held at Launceston in 1971 had drawn up a policy on Aborigines which stated (according to press releases):

1. The Office of Aboriginal Affairs to be upgraded to ministerial level and the Commonwealth to assume the ultimate responsibility for Aborigines and Islanders accorded it by the Referendum of 1967. Labor will evolve ways to regularly consult representatives of Aboriginal and Island people as to their wishes when policies are being developed and legislation prepared.
2. Aborigines to have equal rights and opportunities with all other Australians, and every form of discrimination against Aborigines to be ended.
3. Aborigines to receive the standard rate of wages for the job and to receive the same industrial protection as other Australians.

Special provisions for employment to be provided in regions where they reside.

4. Educational opportunities to be provided in no way inferior to those of the general community, with special programmes at all levels where necessary to overcome cultural deprivation and meet special needs. Pre-school education to be provided for every Aboriginal child including teaching indigenous languages where desirable. Adult education to be provided as broadly as possible.
5. Labor to give priority to a vigorous housing scheme in order to properly house all Aboriginal families within a period of ten years. In compensation for the loss of traditional lands funds will be made available to assist Aborigines who wish to purchase their own homes; the personal wishes of Aborigines as to design and location will be taken into account.
6. A health offensive to be launched to eliminate leprosy, yaws, hookworm, tuberculosis and contagious diseases and to reduce infant mortality. Efficient mortality statistics to be maintained to measure the effectiveness of these policies among Aborigines.
7. Aborigines to have the right to receive social services in the same way as all other Australians.
8. All Aboriginal lands to be vested in a public trust or trusts composed of Aborigines or Islanders as appropriate. Exclusive corporate land rights will be granted to Aboriginal communities which retain a strong tribal structure or demonstrate a potential for corporate action in regard to land at present reserved for the use of Aborigines, or where traditional occupancy according to tribal custom can be established from anthropological or other evidence. No Aboriginal lands shall be alienated except with the approval both of the trust and of Parliament. Aboriginal land rights shall carry with them full rights to minerals in those lands. The sacred sites of the Aborigines will be mapped and protected.
9. Australia to ratify International Labor Conventions No. 107 (The Indigenous and Tribal Population Convention, 1957) and No. 111 (The Discrimination, Employment and Occupation

Convention, 1958) and these Conventions to apply to all indigenous peoples under Australian authority.

10. A parliamentary committee to be established to study all aspects of policy and report to Parliament regularly and continuously.
11. Every Australian child to be taught the history and culture of Aboriginal and Island Australians as an integral part of the history of Australia.
12. Trained social workers to be provided in every area where housing of Aborigines has been undertaken.

The Conference also adopted a series of resolutions of which several were relevant to Aborigines:

Aboriginal Representation: Labor will provide special representation of Aboriginal members of the Legislative Council of the Northern Territory. The provision of Aboriginal representation in state and federal parliaments is referred to the Legal and Constitutional Committee with the request that they find legal and constitutional steps necessary to achieve such representation and recommend them to the next Conference.

Reserves and Settlements: The Queensland Branch ALP wishes to draw to the attention of the Federal Conference the shocking living and working conditions now existing at Bamaga on the northern-most tip of the Cape York Peninsula, in relation to wages, cost of living, etc., and asks the Federal Parliamentary Labor Party to act urgently to force Commonwealth action to remedy the distressing situation that exists on this Queensland government reserve and further requests that the Federal Parliamentary Labor Party seek Commonwealth intervention to improve conditions on all native reserves and settlements.

Gurindji Land Rights: That efforts be made through the appropriate channels to have the Gurindji claim to their ancestral land brought before the United Nations.

In his policy speech to the nation before the election, Mr Whitlam said:

> We will legislate to give Aborigines land rights — not just because their case is beyond argument, but because all of

> us as Australians are diminished while the Aborigines are denied their rightful place in the nation.

Further in the policy speech Mr Whitlam said that a Labor government would override Queensland's discriminatory laws, pay the legal costs for Aborigines in all proceedings in all courts and:

Legislate to establish, for land in Commonwealth territories which is reserved for Aboriginal use and benefit, a system of Aboriginal tenure based on the traditional rights of clans and other tribal groups and, under this legislation, vest such land in Aboriginal communities;

Invite the governments of Western Australia and South Australia to join with the Commonwealth in establishing a Central Australian Aboriginal Reserve (including Ayers Rock and Mount Olga) under the control of Aboriginal trustees;

Establish an Aboriginal Land Fund to purchase or acquire land for significant continuing Aboriginal communities and to appropriate $5 million per year to this fund for the next ten years;

Legislate to prohibit discrimination on grounds of race, ratify all the relevant United Nations and ILO Conventions for this purpose, and set up conciliation procedures to promote understanding and cooperation between Aboriginal and other Australians;

Legislate to enable Aboriginal communities to be incorporated for their own social and economic purposes.

Added Mr Whitlam:

> Let us never forget this; Australia's real test as far as the rest of the world, and particularly our region is concerned, is the role we create for our own Aborigines. In this sense, and it is a very real sense, the Aborigines are our true link with our region … Australia's treatment of her Aboriginal people will be the thing upon which the rest of the world will judge Australia and Australians not just now, but in the greater perspective of history … The Aborigines are a responsibility we cannot escape, cannot share, cannot shuffle off; the world will not let us forget that.

So, the blacks were plumping for Labor (and of course, praying that they would lose Howson). When the general euphoria had died down the obvious question was, 'Are Labor's land rights only for the northern tribal people and not for the de-tribalised southerners who have suffered the worst at the hands of the white man?'

There had already been a number of black attempts to formulate a cohesive land claim. FCAATSI, in 1969, had claimed:

1. Aboriginal ownership of existing reserves.
2. Recognition of Aboriginal ownership of traditional tribal lands at present owned and leased by the Crown.
3. Aboriginal consent for, and benefit from, mining and other development on all Aboriginal land.
4. Establishment of an Aboriginal land claims court to facilitate the awarding of compensation to Aborigines wherever Aboriginal land is alienated.
5. Setting up of a National Aboriginal Land Trust Fund to accept and allocate compensation or rent for all the land of Australia which had been alienated from the Aboriginal owners.

In April 1971 Justice Blackburn of the Northern Territory Supreme Court had given his judgement in the *Gove Land Rights* case. Astonishingly, this was the first important case in Australia to be concerned with 'land rights' or to involve Aborigines as plaintiffs. In 1968 the Commonwealth government granted a mineral lease to the Nabalco consortium enabling it to mine bauxite on the Gove Peninsula, an area included in the Arnhem Land Aboriginal Reserve (declared in 1931). The Aboriginal people from Yirrkala, a settlement within the area leased, claimed various proprietary rights to the land in the area and alleged that the rights of 'native communities to land within territory acquired by the Crown' could not be terminated except by their consent or 'perhaps by explicit legislation'. They argued that their ancestors were, under Aboriginal 'law and custom', entitled to the land in 1788 and that their rights had not since been validly extinguished by the Crown. In the event it was held that the ordinance granting the lease was in fact valid legislation and this in itself defeated the Yirrkala people's claim, but a great many other issues were aired. The following discussion of some aspects of the case is put together with the help of several legal acquaintances.

The plaintiffs, representing thirteen clans (patrilineal descent groups), anthropologists and others gave evidence of the nature of Aboriginal 'law and custom'. The judge recognised the existence of a 'subtle and elaborate' system of Aboriginal Law 'highly adapted to the country in which the people led their lives' but nevertheless held that he was bound by legal precedent to consider the black claim in terms of the (British) common law concept of 'property'. He defined that concept to include three elements — the right to alienate (that is, to dispose of an interest in property), the right to exclude others and the right to 'use and enjoy' — but indicated that it might not be necessary to establish all of them or to establish them without qualification.

The plaintiffs could clearly not satisfy the first element. As I pointed out earlier, Aboriginal land was held collectively and inalienably by groups (clans) to whom that land and its sacred sites was the source of spiritual well-being. On the second element, the court was unconvinced by evidence presented that the clans in fact had a right to exclude those who were not members from their land. On the third element, it was indicated in evidence that hunting and food-gathering (the economic use of the land) was carried out not by the clan as such but by a group of fluctuating membership that has been called by anthropologists a 'horde' or 'band'. The court held that although the plaintiff clans had a 'religious' connection with the land this had 'little significance in the economic sense'. Evidence was given by anthropologists that the 'band' normally consisted mainly of people of the same clan and that it normally stayed on that clan's land but the judge was not convinced of this from the evidence of Aboriginal witnesses.

And so the clans were not able to establish even in principle that the highly organised society that occupied, identified with and lived off the land in 1788, and had presumably done so for millennia before, asserted any 'proprietary' rights to it at all!

Even in terms of the common law concept of 'property' (and leaving aside for the moment the *moral* injustice of the common law invoking it in the first place), it appears that the clans failed on this point on what are, in commonsense terms, technicalities. What practical differences does it make whether the land was 'economically' exploited by 'bands' or 'clans'? Is it impossible for the common law, even as it stands, to recognise the complete interdependence of the 'religious' and 'economic' elements of traditional Aboriginal life? The Aboriginal ethic of hospitality meant in practice that no clan would exclude neighbouring groups from the *peaceful* use of its own land for food-gathering purposes (though they *did* exclude others from sacred sites), even if it could. Such an attitude reflects the social and economic reality of a harsh environment. Why can it not reasonably be regarded simply as a qualification of the right to 'exclude others', if that is what must be established? But of course in *commonsense* terms it is to begin with both absurd and unjust to rely on a legal concept (with all its social overtones of competition, privacy, etc.) that was unknown to Aboriginal Law.

The judge also considered the question of whether British common law in 1788 or afterwards recognised the doctrine of 'communal native title' in Aboriginal Law, which the plaintiffs were attempting to establish. After considering a large number of cases, including many decided in the USA, Canada, New Zealand, India and Africa he held that the common law itself did not recognise 'native' title and that such recognition had always been the result of 'statute or executive policy'. A number of early US cases in particular seemed to hold some hope for Aborigines but the judge thought that more recent cases there had overruled the doctrine if it had ever existed. He quoted a passage from *Tee-Hit-Ton Indians* v. *US* (1955) 348 US 222, in which it was said that:

> It is well settled that in all States of the Union the tribes who inhabit the lands of the States held claim to such lands after the coming of the white man under what is sometimes called original native title or permission from the whites to occupy. That description means mere possession not

> recognised as ownership by Congress. After conquest they were permitted to occupy portions of territory over which they had previously exercised 'sovreignty' [sic] as we use that term. This is not a property right but amounts to an occupancy which the sovreign grants and protects against exclusion from third parties [i.e. *other* subjects of the Crown] but which rights of occupancy may be terminated and such lands fully disposed of by the sovreign itself without any legally enforced obligation to compensate the Indians.

After citing various authorities, the judge in addition held that he was obliged to adopt the 'legal fiction' that the white occupation of Australia was in the nature of a settlement of a deserted, uncultivated land — that Australia was not 'conquered'! In that circumstance the common law holds that all English laws that are applicable are immediately in force. (In a 'conquered' colony indigenous law remains in force until it is specifically altered.) Yet the court at the same time held that the Yirrkala people had not satisfactorily established that their own ancestors had actually occupied the land in question, commenting that the evidence presented was based on 'mythological' rather than historical explanation!

There are legal and 'anthropological' as well as moral arguments against many aspects of this decision. Other courts and other circumstances may bring changes to the common law as it apparently exists in Australia but Justice Blackburn was in some ways quite liberal in the approach he took to the case and it is obvious that the only real hope for the recognition of land rights is in government action.

And in the area of 'statute or executive policy' the governments for instance of the USA, Canada and New Zealand have been far ahead of Australia (notwithstanding the inadequacies of their policies*). It was established as a matter of

* e.g. The title to Indian reservations in the USA and Canada is held in trust by government agencies and this gives the agencies great power over the tribal governments. The resulting paternalistic policies are partly the cause of the resentments among grassroots Indians that found expression at Wounded Knee.

principle (often abused in practice), in North America before the white settlement of Australia began and in New Zealand by the Treaty of Waitangi in 1840, that land was to be alienated from the Aboriginal inhabitants only with their 'consent' and in return for payment. By 1945 the US government for example, had paid about 800 million dollars to the Indians for land purchase and in 1946 Congress set up the Indian Claims Commission to deal with outstanding claims and to 'correct any mistakes' in previous transactions.

The Commission is empowered to consider:

1. Claims arising under the Constitution, laws and treaties of the USA;
2. All other claims which would arise if the US government could be sued;
3. Claims which would be made if agreements made with the government over the years were revised on the basis of fraud, mistake, unfair pressure etc.;
4. Claims based on the fact that compensation for lands taken from the Indians has not been paid for at rates agreed by the Indians;
5. Claims based upon moral arguments as to what is fair and honourable irrespective of what the law has to say on the matter.

The last head gives the Commission the widest possible legal jurisdiction. In effect it has the power to make judgements based on its estimate of what is a fair thing for the Indians concerned. It can exercise the power even if the claim is covered by other laws or principles established in the United States.†

But as A. Barrie Pittock could write before the last federal election (in *Racism in Australia*, Volume 2, edited by Frank Stevens),

† Nevertheless, there has been much dissatisfaction with the length of time taken in the hearing of claims and in the fact that as much as twenty per cent of the amounts awarded have been taken up in legal fees.

> The question of recognising an Aboriginal right to land, or compensation for land, not presently reserved for Aborigines, but which was alienated from them at some time in the past, has not received serious attention from any Australian government ... No part of Australia ... has yet been purchased from Aborigines by the Crown.

As Pittock also points out, this attitude is contradicted by the eighty-year-old Australian government policy of recognising indigenous land rights in Papua (and in New Guinea when that became an Australian mandated territory). He was of course writing before December 1972 but we have yet to see exactly what Labor will in practice do about the matter.

In 1966 the South Australian government (followed by Victoria (1970), New South Wales and Western Australia (1972)) recognised Aboriginal title to existing reserves (elsewhere they remain merely Crown land) but this is of direct benefit only to those Aborigines who live on the reserves and the areas involved are in any case minuscule. As I said in Chapter 2, in my own lifetime large areas formerly reserved in New South Wales have been quietly put to other uses without reference to the people living there.

Existing schemes in the Northern Territory, Queensland and Western Australia providing for payment of a royalty on minerals taken from Aboriginal reserves into a trust fund for the benefit of Aborigines in the state or territory involved are perhaps better than nothing, but they are hardly an adequate substitute for full rights of ownership and self-determination.

Since coming out of jail in June 1971, I had been gathering the opinions of Aborigines from various states about the land claim. Soon after the Embassy was set up, I travelled to Melbourne in company with Pastor Frank Roberts of the (then) New South Wales Aboriginal Land Board (a black organisation) to attend an Abschol meeting convened to discuss land. With the help of a panel of legal experts there, we drafted a rough prototype setting out approximate grounds of the land claim which would later be formulated into a bill of legislation.

The Aboriginal Land Rights Bill was drawn up so as to cover the whole of Australia including the territories (excluding Papua), the Torres Strait Islands and all states. The main points are as follows:

All land has been stolen from Aborigines, therefore Aborigines demand from the government:

- the return of all 'crown lands' recognised as Aboriginal reserves.
- that these reserves be deeded in perpetuity to the Aboriginal people and administered by them.
- that any 'Crown lands' which are of traditional or sacred significance to Aborigines be deeded to them in perpetuity.
- that all sites of anthropological or traditional significance discovered apart from on reserves or 'Crown lands' be preserved and made accessible to Aborigines.
- that all hunting and fishing rights and areas be open to the use of Aborigines without fee or constraint.
- that where Aborigines have been removed from land reserves in accordance with government land alienation policies and otherwise, fair land compensation grants be made, preferably from established 'Crown lands' or areas bought by governments in reparation, to restore a land base to Aborigines and to purchase additional suitable land for Aborigines.
- that Aborigines in each state be given corporate ownership and control of all reserves.
- that all such lands be exempt from the provisions of the relevant mining acts.
- that in these areas, ownership rights be granted over minerals to corporate Aboriginal groups so as to give them effective priority in prospecting and mining rights.
- that no mineral exploration or exploitation occur in Aboriginal areas without prior consultation and approval by local Aborigines.
- that as an act of compensation for the loss of all other parts of the continent, a national Aborigines Trust Fund for Aboriginal developments and enterprise be established.

This is to be reparation and under Aboriginal administrative control and to be in addition to normal government assistance to Aborigines as Australian citizens.

The draft contents for the Bill are as follows:

1. The Bill will commence with a statement in principle which recognises Aboriginal land rights. The Canadian Bill provides a model for this.
2. The Bill will provide for the establishment in each state, and one for the territories, of an Aboriginal Land Trust which will consist of twelve members elected by Aborigines from that particular state or territory. (The function of the State Land Trust will be to hold title to the land vested in it. Aboriginal ownership of this land will be in perpetuity, however, there should be an ability to lease provided in the act. [Note, lease but *not* sale.])
3. The land that the Aboriginal Land Trust will hold will be:
   (a) All land presently reserved for the use and benefit of Aboriginal people; i.e. all reserves in that particular state or territory.
   (b) Title to a land grant to each Aboriginal Land Trust, the size of the land grant being:

$$\frac{\text{\% of dispossessed Aborigines in each state}}{\text{Total population of state}} \times \frac{\text{Area of state}}{1}$$

   (c) Sites which are of traditional, sacred or historical significance to Aborigines.
   (d) Customary Land — land traditionally and/or currently occupied by Aboriginal groups not living on reserves. This land to be bought by government and returned to Aboriginal Land Trust ownership.
   (e) Any land subsequently purchased by each Land Trust.
4. The Bill will provide for the establishment of a National Aboriginal Development Commission. The Commission will be constituted by the appointment from each Aboriginal Land

Trust of two of its members to serve on the Commission. The Commission's function will be to hold compensation monies made out to Aboriginal groups and to act as a financing body for Aboriginal development. It will hand over funds to State Aboriginal Lands Trusts for small scale development projects within that state. The Commission will directly fund or raise finance for large scale or national development projects.

(All Aboriginal Trusts, Commissions etc. must be independent of and outside the public service structure. The public service, by virtue of its authoritarian nature, will inevitably nullify any glad new hope, any dawning for the Aboriginal race.)

5. The Bill will provide for the appointment by each Land Trust of adjudicators of disputes between Aboriginal groups on claims to compensation and to land title under the customary land and sites section of the Bill.
6. The Bill will provide for the establishment of Aboriginal Land Tribunals for each state or territory which will hear claims for land title under the customary and sites section of the Bill and fix compensation. The Tribunal will be constituted by four persons appointed by the Aboriginal Land Trust and three persons appointed by the Commonwealth of Australia — who are acceptable to the Aboriginal people.
7. Compensation will be fixed as the value of land taken from Aboriginal groups at the time of taking, 1770, calculated at the English land upset price of that time, plus interest on this, together with an inflation factor (to be set by the Commonwealth Statistician).
8. The Bill will provide for no federal, state or local taxation for land held by Land Trusts, except land that is income-earning land, that income-earning land to be tax free for fifty years and this provision to be examined at the end of this time.
9. State Land Trusts and the National Aboriginal Development Commission will be exempt from income tax for the first fifty years and this provision to be examined at the end of this time.
10. *Mining:* The Western Australian act provides the model here. Bill also to include *timber* rights — only relevant for

Commonwealth territories, with provision for complementary state legislation.

The Bill should provide for the turning over to each Land Trust an amount equal to 1/12 of the state or territory Aboriginal welfare budget for the repurchase of land which is to be added to present reserve lands to make them viable economic units. This provision to operate for ten years.

The purpose of corporate ownership, holding land in perpetuity with the right of sale withheld and the right of lease given, is apparent. So is the need to withhold compensation monies from waste by irresponsible individuals who will achieve nothing of value with the money paid to them. Under customary Aboriginal possessory title, the land belonged to, indeed was a spiritual part of, the people. It could not be sold or bartered and by this fact it was ensured that the land would remain with its locally identified group. And so it should remain in perpetuity under corporate ownership, so that for all time Aborigines will remain in possession of land identity and retain a land base.

Should the Aboriginal group in any area pass away, or relinquish that area, those lands will still remain in corporate title as Aboriginal land and a lease system will apply with revenue going to a central fund. The Aboriginal Land Trust will decide if it is to be used by Australians generally as a national park or wildlife reserve so that the title may live on immemorially while best serving the Aboriginal identity with that area and also serving to act as a partial brake on man's greed — the greed that is slowly encroaching on Australia's parklands and public areas while leaving insufficient natural land, fauna and flora for the enjoyment and appreciation of coming generations.

When the Embassy was set up, I had particularly asked the then 'Ambassador' and staff *not* to make any detailed statement about land. This was because I felt that no black having to make land claim, within the Australian legal system and without some knowledge of international precedents on native possessory rights, was able to do so without first getting help from legal advisers. It should've been apparent from the *Gove Land Rights* case that blacks could not rely on the law as it stood. It is difficult territory and there is no shame for blacks to admit that they need help in traversing it.

The accursed parole restrictions kept me well and truly out of Canberra all the time the Embassy was standing and, of course, at the time that the land claim was to be released. Simultaneously, all that smacked of Gilbert was rapidly being frozen out of Aboriginal affairs both on the radical and conservative levels because I had started publicly criticising some of the gutlessness and/or abuses that were current at the Foundation for Aboriginal Affairs, *Identity* magazine and the Embassy. It wasn't appreciated (although I must record in passing that in two of these cases the point was later taken and partial reforms introduced. The third looks to be well and truly on the skids.) My criticism of the conduct of several Embassy notables however ensured that the Abschol draft of the land claim was not put forward by the Embassy. This wouldn't have mattered if a little more homework had been done on the land claim that *was* released:

1. Establishment of the Northern Territory as a state within the Commonwealth of Australia, and the parliament of the Northern Territory to be mainly Aboriginal in composition, with title and mining rights to all land within the territory.
2. Legal and mining rights to all other presently existing reserve lands and settlements throughout Australia.
3. Preservation of all sacred sites throughout Australia.
4. Legal title and mining rights to areas in and around Australian capital cities.
5. Compensation monies for lands not returnable to take the form of down-payments amounting to six billion dollars, and an annual percentage of the gross national income …

Nobody could say that the young blacks who dreamt this one up weren't enthusiastic and at the time it probably made them feel better as well. One can only wish that this official claim had been a little less of the stuff that dreams are made of and a little more capable of attracting serious consideration by the Australian nation. I am not arguing against the moral foundation for the Embassy land/compensation claims — just its practical logic. Australian blacks are not bargaining from a position of strength so why not keep within the realms of what can be achieved? For example, Aboriginal women are raped or used as sex objects all over the continent. One day it will be possible for blacks to organise vigilante forces to prevent this. These things in the foreseeable future are possibilities and hence warrant serious consideration. The formation of a land-army of blacks (1% of the population) to take on the Australian Army is quite another thing — so why waste time discussing it?

Of course the Liberal–Country Party boys loved the Embassy's land claim and Interior Minister Hunt made considerable capital out of it in his subsequent anti-black propaganda booklet. In retrospect, the Embassy contributed nothing to the Aboriginal land claim in terms of theoretical detail. Its contribution and its historical importance lay rather in the fact that it put the *idea* of land claim well and truly in the news. The need for a nation-wide black conference to thresh out the land claim issue thoroughly is obvious. Blacks organise land conferences here and there whenever they are able to. They are never properly representative because very few blacks can afford to travel. To have a representative and decisive national black conference on the land issue would take funding on a scale that only a government could sustain. It is the old question all over again — blacks haven't got the money and the whites are not likely to support such a conference on the scale needed. Frustration roll on ...

5

Labor's Santa Claus

The record of Labor man Gordon Bryant's first months in office is undeniably impressive and gives an indication of the amount of energy and idealism that Labor has brought to Aboriginal affairs. It is a pity that blacks are not aware of just what has already been achieved. The following list may not be complete because just before deadline day there was a postal mix-up which ensured that I stopped receiving the ministerial press releases for a while.

Nevertheless the following gives a good idea of recent developments and announcements:

14/12/72	Aboriginal children in tribal communities to be given their primary education in their own language (so implementing both ILO and UNESCO conventions relating to the teaching of indigenous peoples in their own languages).
21/12/72	$103,000 for eight grants in the various states to further Aboriginal projects.
22/12/72	Purchase of Panter Downs, a 440,000 acre pastoral property north-east of Derby, Western Australia, for the use of the Aboriginal community at Mowanjum.
date unknown	$100,000 from the Commonwealth Capital Fund for Aboriginal Enterprises to buy shares in a company being formed to market the produce from more than sixty turtle and crocodile farms being developed in

northern Australia by Aborigines and Islanders. Shares held by the Fund to be vested in incorporated bodies of Aboriginals and Islanders as soon as practicable.

10/1/73 $10.85 million extra allowed for Aboriginal advancement projects.

1/2/73 Bryant puts forward proposals for a 100 man Aboriginal field force; about one man for every 1000 Aborigines, to be stationed all over Australia to facilitate the process of consultation with blacks.

16/2/73 An increase in the number of Aboriginal housing associations in the Northern Territory to be encouraged. Eventual aim: to do away with Aboriginal housing via the bureaucratic system, so that ultimately the association could handle it all.

26/2/73 $35,000 for 286,000 acre property, Mount Minnie, near Onslow, Western Australia, for the use of the Noualla group of Aborigines.

8/3/73 $90,000 to relieve acute housing shortage for Aborigines at Oodnadatta; money to go through Oodnadatta Housing Association — a black group.

9/3/73 Agreement on proposals to finance the extension of existing Aboriginal legal services throughout Australia.

25/3/73 $55,000 grant to support a newly formed Aboriginal and Islander Community Health Service in Brisbane.

6/4/73 Formal offer to states for Commonwealth to take over all responsibility for policy and planning programmes for Australian Aborigines. (This will probably be a *fait-accompli* by the time this book appears.)

10/4/73 Government to establish an Aboriginal Land Fund to buy or acquire land *outside* reserves for Aboriginal communities. It to allow for an expenditure of $5 million a year.

12/4/73 Federal Minister for Health announces a national conference 'next year' to discuss the health of Aborigines and their situation in each state. (In May, the AMA announced that it would help the

	Commonwealth in measures to improve Aboriginal health.)
21/4/73	Purchase of a 1.2 million acre cattle station, Willowra Station, Northern Territory, for Aboriginal use. The minister voiced fears of a 'white backlash' over this purchase, because 'racial intolerance was imbedded deep in some communities'.
22/4/73	$50,000 grant to enable an Islander Co-operative on Thursday Island to establish a large-scale fishing enterprise.
9/5/73	$125,000 for the purchase of two properties totalling 983 acres adjacent to Cummeragunga Aboriginal Reserve near Echuca.
24/5/73	$45,000 grant to Inger Rice Foundation (to promote mother and child care).
May	$530,000 to Redfern's Aboriginal Community Housing Project.

Whatever blacks in the northern parts of Australia may have been thinking, it must be recorded that every black to whom I spoke in the south was hoping that Jim Keeffe would become Minister for Aboriginal Affairs in the new government. Over and over again he had shown himself to be a champion of black causes. His relationship with the Embassy blacks was excellent and any matter referred to him either in person or by letter by blacks has received prompt and courteous attention. Minister-elect Bryant, though experienced in Aboriginal affairs by dint of having been FCAATSI's vice-president for over seventeen years was, in many eyes condemned precisely because of this connection with FCAATSI, which has never been a representative body. Blacks feared that through Bryant, it would come to call the tune to black affairs.

Anyway, Bryant it was and after meeting him, and more importantly, observing his performance to date, it does appear to me the choice was a good one. He takes an overwhelming, hand-rubbing, grinning delight in being minister. He is not a boiled shirt and the man's gleeful sincerity and relish in his job is obvious. All in all a welcome change from the mean-eyed self-importance of some of the Aboriginal affairs ministers at state and federal level of recent years.

On December 15 last year [1972], Prime Minister Whitlam had announced the appointment of Mr Justice Woodward as Commissioner to conduct a judicial enquiry as a first move towards the legal recognition of Aboriginal rights in land. Land rights was already government policy, but Justice Woodward was to advise on *how* they should be granted or vested in Aboriginal communities. Justice Woodward had been counsel for the Aboriginal community at Yirrkala and had obtained extensive experience and understanding of traditional forms of Aboriginal land holding during his conduct of the *Gove Land Rights* case. His terms of reference were:

(a) arrangements for vesting title to land in the Northern Territory of Australia now reserved for the use and benefit of the Aboriginal inhabitants of that territory, including rights in minerals and timber, in an appropriate body or bodies, for granting rights in or in relation to that land to the Aboriginal groups or communities concerned with that land;
(b) the desirability of establishing suitable procedures for the examination of claims to Aboriginal traditional rights and interests in or in relation to land in areas in the Northern Territory of Australia outside Aboriginal reserves or of establishing alternative ways of meeting effectively the needs for land of Aboriginal groups or communities living outside those reserves;
(c) the effect of already existing commitments, whether in the nature of Crown leases, government contracts, mining rights or otherwise, on the attainment of the objects of recognising Aboriginal traditional rights and interests in or in relation to land;
(d) the changes in legislation required to give effect to the recommendations arising from (a), (b) and (c) above; and
(e) such other matters relating to rights and interests of the Aborigines in or in relation to land as may be referred to

the Aboriginal Land Rights Commission by the Minister of Aboriginal Affairs.

On January 11, Mr Bryant announced plans to establish a committee of Aborigines to advise the government. The inaugural meeting of the Interim National Aboriginal Consultative Committee was held in Canberra on February 21–3.

By late February, blacks were becoming restive, both about the Consultative Committee and the Woodward appointment. The government had stressed, right from the start, that consultation with blacks was central to its thinking. Yet the appointment of Justice Woodward was accomplished without any consultation whatsoever. Blacks felt that no white Australian, no matter how experienced, could recommend on land justice. Many felt that a black jurist or jurists from a neutral country should have been sought for the job and that Aborigines should serve on the Land Rights Commission as well. Clearly it was another case of blacks 'being done to.' Also, Aborigines questioned the restriction of land rights to Aborigines in the Northern Territory only and also the manner of formation of the Consultative Committee. Said Chicka Dixon apropos the Labor Party's moves:

> There is no true representation, no true consultation. The same old heads that were on the Liberal Party's committee are now on the Consultative Committee. Only the Libs called it the Advisory Committee. They've just changed the name. But the same old Toms are on it. So what they've got to do, in my opinion, is to get rid of them and put in grassroots blacks. If you cut this state up into four areas, or eight, and get true representation it'd be a different thing. Looking at those black heads at that Consultative Committee — most of them were working for government before! Most of them haven't a worry in the world. *They* live in nice homes with no worries about where the next feed is coming from. So it's not a good, clear, honest black voice!

Just because there's a change of government, a lot of blacks think that the Labor government is going to solve all their problems. The 'Toms' are going to sit back and let the Labor Party go on its merry way. Now I'm not prepared to do that and there's quite a few blacks who think like me — that we've got to keep on hammering. They think that just because they've set up that bloody fiasco, the Consultative Committee, blacks will keep quiet. And Bryant said there'd be 100 blacks working in the field. Now that's just tokenism. I asked him 'What are you going to do about the infant mortality rate? You were good in Opposition, talking about it. You know what it is; let's clean it up!' I even went further. I said 'Let's be hypothetical. If it were ten white babies dying for every one black, what would happen?' He got a silly grin on his face. He knows what would happen! They'd go at it with heaps of bloody experts and qualified medical staff and clean the problem up.

He probably *is* seeking answers to the problems. He'd do better if he stopped flying here and there and listened instead to grassroots opinion. They may not have BAs and MAs and so forth after their names, but they certainly know what they want. Until such time as they do sit down with blacks at the grassroots level, I don't think they're ever going to solve the problem. It seems to me that since the inception of white government in this country, no blacks have ever sat down with any political party and *formed* policy. None.

And Bobbi Sykes:

I don't think that *any* white Australian can be thought to be impartial on the issue of the Aboriginal land claim. I would say, further, that judging by Judge Woodward's history, he is definitely not the person to do it — besides being an Australian, which automatically makes him biased in favour of white Australians — or in this particular instance it certainly does. He's never been involved in a civil rights issue, he has no idea of how blacks think about things and he has, on many occasions, been on the side of the employers. I see that having gone through that, it becomes habitual that you think in this way. To identify with the oppressor rather than the oppressed. I don't think that his one little flutter into the arena of working on behalf of blacks could be said to constitute an interest on behalf of blacks. In order to prove to me, at least, that they were really genuine, Labor's first step would've been to re-open the Yirrkala land case. And they would've made finance available for blacks to hire whoever they felt they would've needed to represent their cause. In my opinion, of course, a person who has had past experience at civil rights law, past experience at land rights cases, would have been an ideal person. Such as an American Indian with experience in this kind of thing and who has no vested interests in Australia. Only such a person could be considered impartial and unbiased. The Yirrkala should've been able to hire whom they liked. Anyone can hire expertise.

Paul Coe:

On land rights, the government have left themselves a very, very good way out by saying that land rights is applicable only by proving tribal association with the land. Now it seems to me absurd to expect people in New South Wales to prove tribal association with the land when the express policy has been, over a period of eighty odd years, with the mission set up, to destroy Aboriginal culture and particularly tribal association with the land. Now in most areas this has been effective. It is absurd to suggest that people can just chuck off eighty years of colonial suppression and re-define their tribal association with the land. The federal government says that it will give land rights to the tribal people because they know that they only have to make a few token gestures. I think that's as far as they are prepared to go and I think that's what they had in mind when they made the statement.

Bryant and Whitlam haven't given the Aboriginal people a voice at all. If Aborigines did have a true voice, there'd be Aboriginal people elected *by* the people. They'd ensure that voter registration drives were undertaken immediately so that all Aboriginal people were given the opportunity to vote, to elect the man of their choice.

In a statement to *The Australian* (3/4/73) Paul also pointed out that when the Alaskan Eskimos and the American Indians were given land rights, they were consulted and had powers of review over all legislation. An Aboriginal body should be set up, with powers to review all legislation that affects Aboriginals, before it is passed. But, Coe added, 'we've heard nothing more about it'.

On March 5, Gordon Bryant gave an address at the Newcastle Trades and Labour Council's Workers' Club which, part reproduced here, answered some of the above questions:

> The situation of the Aboriginal people of Australia is a national disgrace. There's no other way to describe it. There are a number of us here tonight who have been around a bit. We know what it's like in various parts of the country. We know that there are people living in tribal areas who are absolutely neglected. We know that there are people living miserably in urban situations — and all the rest of it. Even though I've been associated with it for years and been around and about and up and down, when suddenly you come upon it, this situation, as a minister, you are appalled at what the situation is — at the situation as you find it. The reason I am more appalled, now, than I was before I was minister, I suppose, is that you realise that, once you reach this exalted station, that there are a lot of resources at your disposal if you have the wit and the will to put them to work. That so much of this is inexcusable. For instance, a few weeks ago, I was at

a place called Papunya which is about 140 miles north-west of Alice Springs. There were about a 1000 people there — some of whom only came in out of the desert four or five years ago. And there they are, in miserable humpies, in miserable conditions — I just don't know how they cook any food — with the awfully inadequate services such as the water supply, the toilets and so on, totally inadequate, and nothing, despite what has been said, is being done to develop the place. And yet, back at Alice Springs, where we landed at the airport — airports are a status symbol in our society — the lawns are green, there's a swimming pool, the buildings are just first class, and all the rest of it. You couldn't believe that Papunya is on the same continent, operated and controlled (or should be) by the same government as developed Canberra. So that, I think, is the first message you've got to give to the people of Australia — that a great deal of the situation in which the Aboriginal people of Australia find themselves is inexcusable. But none of us know the answers to social questions, whether people are black or white. We can only hope though, that when the material conditions in which people find themselves are altered, as they can be, easily, by governments, things will improve. And I think if there's anything that I've got to say to the people of Australia, it's that this has got to change. That no matter what you look at, whether it is the material conditions or all the other things in society — we've neglected the Aboriginal people … I don't know what the figures are [regarding the] housing situation of the Aboriginal people of Australia, but I should guess that something between 20 to 30,000 people, Aboriginal people, live in miserable housing, inadequate housing.

Then there's the health situation. Over the whole area of health — child health, maternal care, the health of elderly people and all the rest of it, the lot of the Aboriginal people is worse than that of the rest of the community and there's a lot of reasons for this.

When we look at the field of education — we've had compulsory education in Australia for 100 years — how many Aboriginal university graduates are there? How many are at universities and tertiary education institutions this year? Perhaps between thirty or forty — I'm not sure of the figures just yet. That's one for every 3 or 4000 of the Aboriginal people in Australia. But in Australia generally it'd be one in every 100 or so. So you've got thirty or forty times more chance to get into a university if you're not an Aborigine than if you are an Aborigine.

On employment. The Aboriginal people, of course, live in those parts of Australia where employment is difficult. Nobody, any more, wants to shift people around — especially the Aboriginal people who have a right to stop where they are — and therefore we have to find new areas of employment. And when you look at employment it's usually employment at the lowest possible levels. In many parts of Australia the Aborigines are still paid less than the award rates.

Then there's the question of community services. Now we live in a community that over a 100 years ago, or, just on 100 years ago, took the overland telegraph line right across Australia … Yet if you go to innumerable Aboriginal communities right across Australia, you find simple things like lack of a telephone service. Papunya, the place I just mentioned — and I use that as my favourite example at the moment because that's a fair sized community, about a 1000 people — nobody's bothered to put telephone communications to there. Now you don't run telephone lines for perhaps 140 miles — or do you? I think the whole of Australia has done so. If it was in a Country Party electorate and there were fifteen Country Party voters then, according to Lionel Bowen's figures, they would have spent about a quarter of a million putting in an automatic exchange for them! And wherever you go around the country, when you drive along and come to the end of the main road, you go another half mile and there's the reserve. The council stopped half a mile back. If you go around the country — the ordinary services — how many medical men are there in communities of that nature? Hardly any at all. So the task we're faced with is changing the whole structure of society and the way it approaches the Aboriginal people. We've got to change community attitudes perhaps — got to change municipal, state and federal governmental agencies and make them get on with the job ... Now I'm not one to say that this situation is anybody in particular's fault. I don't think any of us have been all that good about it all. Up until ten or fifteen years ago there weren't that many noises made about it. Labor governments, Liberal governments, Country Party governments gave up in despair — they didn't try. They said 'Well, you can't do much with them, can you?' And so on.

But there's been a total change in the situation in the last twelve or fifteen years. And Australia has this task on its hands. My predecessors were facing a situation in which most people of the world have been at a loss to find an answer. The small ethnic minorities around the world are all unfortunately in much the same situation. Well, we are out to change it. We can, of course, draw upon the example and lessons from the rest of the world and we are trying to do that. And so, what have we attempted to do so far? First of all, one of the first things we did was [to announce] that concerning Aboriginal people — Aboriginal children in schools which were basically Aboriginal and which were close to their tribal background — [there would be an] attempt to teach them in their tribal language. We received a letter the other day, denouncing this. Well, it's good sound educational practice, to teach people in their native tongue, particularly when they are starting school ...

And then we tackle the question of land rights. Now this is a burning question. Strangely enough, in my experience, it's only become a real question over the last eight or nine years. I can remember when at conferences it started to come up as an alternative to some of the social questions such as housing and changing the legislation. And this means something. Now I think land probably means two different things to the Aboriginal people of Australia. It's got a symbolic meaning to Aboriginal people in urban societies, but its got a spiritual context for all those who live close to the ground in the north of Australia and Western Australia and so on. I've been associated with the campaign of the people of Yirrkala ever since 1963 when it all started. I went in to the court myself in Darwin, on their behalf — probably the first occasion on which someone had done this. It wasn't a question of owning a piece of real estate. It was a case of spiritual repression. I can understand that. You can understand that. We all feel a bit like this about things that are part of our environment. I say to my friends at home, down in the friendly environment of Melbourne, 'What would happen if someone tried to dig up the Melbourne Cricket Ground — you'd get an uproar if you started anything like that. Or the grounds of St Paul's Cathedral, or even St Pat's.' So there you are. We've all got these values ourselves, but we don't expect the Aboriginal people of Australia to have them. We tended, up until recently — now there has been a change — to look upon land as a piece of commercial real estate. The issue was, what are you going to use it for? Smoking factory chimney there, six canneries there, 25,000 sheep there. If you're not doing that, you're wasting it. Of course that's not the way the Aboriginal people look upon land and increasingly, it's not the way the rest of us look upon land. And so we charged Judge Woodward with the task of finding a solution to this question — legally. That is, how is it to be defined? How much is there to be of it? How is it to be arranged? How are we to see that the Aborigines have their land protected? That's probably not all that hard. It wouldn't be all that difficult to fire a law through the House of Representatives and the

Senate setting aside the Aboriginal lands of the Northern Territory for the people in perpetuity. To define how they are to use them, control them and use them for their own employment is in fact a little difficult. But what we're going to do about the landless people of the south and the urban society is something I can't determine — something we'll give him to try and determine — something which people who are here tonight might well have thoughts about. And you should let him know. We'd like to get the people of Australia to sit down and do some steady, solid thinking about this themselves ...

Throughout Australia, our scouts — members of the Department and so on — are examining situations where people feel that they want this piece of land or that piece of land. And it seems to me that we may well be coming to a formula which will help some people, particularly in the remoter parts of Australia where land is not all that hard to get. Where you can buy a fair slice of country for perhaps $35–40,000. For instance, the other week one of our people was over in Onslow in Western Australia. The people there — they're living in a town — have got all the problems of the Aboriginal people all over Australia. The young men drink too much and so do the other people. The place offers a pretty miserable sort of an existence. But out there on their traditional land — 250,000 acres of it ... It's not all that attractive as a piece of terrain if you wanted to set up a farm but it'll run 5–6000 sheep or more. And our man talked to them about it. They said, 'We just want that. If we can get that, we can go out there. We can move out, back to where we came from. And we can go to the town as we require to.' And he came back to ask if he could have permission to negotiate. I told him he did. Then a few telephone calls and the people were ready to sell and we signed on the dotted line then and there. Four or five days after he'd been there it was signed and sealed and it only needed all the conveyancing and so on. And at least we gave them an understanding that the Commonwealth means business. In other places, of course, it's not all that easy. There's one very large piece of land that's held up because it's a family estate and you've got to have fifteen or twenty signatures and there's still three or four to get after four or five months. They're not in Australia, they're somewhere else. So around Australia we're getting pieces of land for people. And wherever it can be done, that's what we will do. Now we're not going to take land off other people at this stage, because other people are entitled to have their feelings about things too.

Then there are all sorts of other operations as well, throughout the country. Helping people get *started* on things. For instance we've just announced $100,000 to the people of Torres Strait in the development of a turtle industry. This can be a very substantial contribution to their welfare. In other parts, for instance, the Western Australian government has handed over the Yandeyarrah station to people who were originally part of Don McLeod's operation over there. In fact they call it 'Don McLeod's mob'. There's two of them now. Now what I see over there in north-western Australia, despite the fact that I think that in parts of Western Australia the situation is worse than anywhere else in Australia, is more self-reliance developing amongst the people for some reason or other — partly because of the way the government has gone about it, partly because of other factors. And so they're moving onto their land and developing things …

Everywhere one comes across matters of some moment which give you great encouragement. Down on the Murray River, there's the Cummeragunga — originally a mission. It is about a 1000 or 1100 acres. About ten or twelve years ago, people such as myself and the Aborigines Advancement League in Victoria started to go up there and encourage the people to do something. Now they were completely broken in spirit. They were completely helpless and lost. And gradually we went along and they bought a few cattle and did a few other things and it was remarkable how little assistance we got out of the state government at *that* time. I won't tell you what its political colour was at that time but I might as well have been dealing with Peter Howson as a matter of fact. Gradually it got under way. A few years ago they got a loan of $65,000 from the Capital Fund. (I believe the Capital Fund charges too much interest and we'll do something about *that* in the near future.) But they fenced the place and they built stockyards and they've got a substantial cattle industry going and with a bit of luck they'll acquire some of the properties next door. Now that place is *totally* different from what it was ten years ago … I stood on top of the rolling hills there and looked across at the pastures that have been developed and the cattle grazing there, sleek and fat, and I knew that in the last six or eight months they'd taken off $12–15,000 in cattle and other production and I knew this despite the fact that they'd put in fifty acres of tomatoes two years running [of which] one got hit by the drought and one got hit by excessive rain. As Kevin Atkinson said to me, 'We must win next time!' Now ten years ago, they didn't even think they could win *anything*. We've got to do that, I think, throughout Australia.

How do we propose to operate? First of all, I believe that the Aboriginal people themselves have got to be brought into the operation. Increasingly around Australia, this, of course, is happening. A week or so ago, in Canberra, I convened a group of people — a national advisory council as I was going to call it. I think it became the National Consultative Committee in the end. It decided its own name. How I looked at it was this. I knew there were dozens of Aboriginal people around Australia who had something to offer. I was certain that it was time to get on with the business. I couldn't take time and have an electoral system which would work throughout Australia. I didn't even know how I'd negotiate about Queensland for instance. I couldn't think, on the spot, as to how you would balance say the small number of people of Victoria against the big numbers in the Northern Territory. And so what I did, I just invited people as I knew them. Some people, I'm sorry now that I didn't invite. But then you just can't get around to all these things. Originally, I thought we'd have about twenty-five or thirty. It grew to forty and then to fifty and I think we had seventy-seven at the finish. I was still inviting people as I met them around Australia three or four days before the conference was convened, to the despair of my staff. That was, people who had been prominent over the years — people whose names came to me — and so on. It wasn't truly representative — it didn't claim to be. There were about, I think, fourteen or fifteen from New South Wales, twenty from Queensland, ten or twelve from Western Australia and about twenty, I think, from the Northern Territory and half a dozen each from Victoria and South Australia and one from Tasmania. (There's still a few left down there.) Their job was to set up a system by which the Aboriginal people can have a representative system of their own. It'll be somewhere around thirty-five or forty people. They've got the job of drawing the electoral boundaries for themselves and deciding it and so on. And they're going to meet again in a few weeks' time and finalise that and then we'll set up a representative advisory council or consultative committee. Then, I hope, we'll be able to give it some teeth — some money, some decisions to make, some actions to take. And that's only part of the business …

On the other side, the structural side, we've applied to the Public Service Board for quite a large field force of Aboriginal people. My own feelings are that it ought to be one for every 1000 Aboriginal folk — say about 100 of them scattered throughout Australia. This would be, say, about fifteen to twenty of them in New South Wales. We could all think of plenty of things for them to do. For every Aboriginal community is beset with all the problems of the rest of society — only more so. And that's the structural approach we have, gradually getting Aboriginal people into the decision-making apparatus wherever we can. Now it is not all that easy. A lot of the things we have to do are highly specialised. You can't administer things just 'out of the blue'. Things don't just turn up. You can't just drop somebody into a position in the Commonwealth Public Service and say 'well, run that George'. So we'll have to have training programmes for people of all ages. I don't believe that we ought to just concentrate on younger people. I'm certain that people in their forties and fifties have a lot to offer if you give them training programmes and so on. In fact this has been the experience in this country after the last war. If people have had twenty or thirty years of their life lost for all sorts of reasons in this way — I know dozens of them all through Australia whom you could take and train to run something or manage something — even perhaps to be teachers or other professional people. Now that's not going to happen overnight. I can wave all the wands I like, but things don't happen right away just because we wave our wands. So we're gradually trying to build up a situation of cooperation with the rest of Australia and the state governments and so on. We're hopeful that the state governments will say, very soon, 'here take it, you handle it'. It's much easier for us to deal with people and do it directly. My own view is that we can't hang around waiting for state governments or municipalities to do things. But we'll go directly to the Aboriginal people and do them ourselves. Some of these will be a bit difficult to organise. But in many cases where there's existing organisations and so on, we'll be able to go straight to it. I believe that government has a direct individual responsibility to people. It's got nothing to do with constitutions or precedents or protocol or anything else. It has to do with what you do in a society when you are dealing with people. As far as I'm concerned, my own staff is concerned and the Department is concerned, there's a direct line of communication from you, or the people, to us. They don't need to go through intermediaries. Now there are some very good intermediaries around, whom we'll exploit, until they come and join us, perhaps. But this is the way it has to be. For too long it has been difficult for Aboriginal people to find answers. To whom do they turn? If they are out the back of Queensland somewhere, do they write to Brisbane and ask them? Well, what's the answer there? Of course, the Queensland government says it *owns* the Aboriginal people. They've got no right to write to anybody else. That's my philosophy of government if I may put it that way.

There's one or two questions that I was asked tonight to deal with. First of all, the new federal grants and proposals for financial aid. The previous government had put fair sized sums aside for all sorts of things, but its whole approach was ad hoc. It just did things as the noises came up. The good old system that the squeaking wheel gets the most grease. Well now in Aboriginal affairs there are many wheels that haven't even got the strength to squeak. And they're the ones with the greatest need, the ones we've got to find. My duty just doesn't run to Newcastle or Purfleet or the Northern Territory. It's the people bereft of everything who one has to find and do something about. So at this moment I'm charged with the responsibility to see that when I come to Newcastle, having been to Sydney and then had communication with Wollongong, that we don't spend all the Commonwealth's national budget on this little bit of Australia … We did allot another $10 million a few weeks ago and that's been made available to the states as opportunity offers. For instance we gave $2.9 million to Queensland. Strangely enough, I didn't get a letter of thanks from Mr Bjelke-Petersen. He was off to the north of Queensland and he said to the Torres Strait Islanders, 'I'll give you $250,000 for housing!' They gave him a round of applause and booed Gough Whitlam! And that's the way politics goes, I suppose …

Now the question has been asked of me about the health situation. I feel this is desperate — I know it's desperate. I started to feel a bit desperate about it myself. How do you get some action taken — out in the north and north-west? How do we get teams of people onto the ground? Well, we've taken this up with my colleague, the Minister for Health and his Department. I have a special consultant on my own staff — on a part-time wage from the ANU. We are developing a programme on which we hope we'll be able to put medical teams or medical stations, you might call them, wherever there are reasonable populations. My own belief is that it doesn't matter if there's only a few hundred. After all, we won't send a ship to sea, if it's got more than a 100 people on it and it's sailing more than 650 miles, without a doctor on it. If you went up to Townsville now, you'd find there's seven or eight doctors in the army establishment up there — one for every 4 or 500 hundred men in an infantry battalion. Some of the toughest and fittest men in Australia — at least that's what the advertisements tell us. And we can do that. But for the Aboriginal people of Australia, we haven't worried all that much. So we're setting up an all-out attack on these particular health and other problems ...

Before I sit down, perhaps I'll say a word about being the government of Australia, or one ninety-third of it or whatever I am ... Australia has at this moment probably a unique governmental system ... of people who have a philosophy worked out, who've spent years struggling to get it accepted and who are now in a position to do it. We are not going to be inhibited by anything. This is a very wealthy country indeed. There's *nothing* that we can't do. I don't agree with the economists who say that productivity is the problem. It isn't ... They can turn out steel by the millions of tons ... We could cover Australia, almost, in women's stockings ... motor tyres and motor cars and television sets. The real problem is the social reorganisation of Australia and that's what we've set out to do. A few weeks ago the Press was saying 'Look what they've done! They've overspent by a $1000 million!' It didn't matter a darn. All that mattered was that some of the people of Australia who had been denied things for a long while were now starting to get them. Money is not the problem. It is the wit and the will and the social organisation. But nothing demonstrates that more than in the Aboriginal situation in Australia. I give you my undertaking that my colleagues and myself are setting out to change it, to improve it and if possible, to find a steady answer. We know that we won't find an answer to the social questions all that easily. But we'll certainly apply all the material resources we can and certainly try and drag out of the Aboriginals themselves and the rest of the community all the intellectual resources necessary to do it.

(Recorded and printed by courtesy of the minister)

Some of the points troubling blacks are adequately answered, some are not. Mr Bryant's explanation for forging on with the Consultative Committee is fair enough. The staff needed to initiate proper voter registration drives amongst blacks all over Australia and then get blacks actually to vote is staggering, as is the time the whole thing would have taken. Had Bryant gone about it this way, there would've been howls from blacks, 'Why isn't he doing more, why is he just sitting back while babies are dying?' As Bryant said in answering a question at Newcastle: 'There are a lot of things you have to do directly. If you are sick, well you get somebody who can make you better. It doesn't matter a damn what his race is, he doesn't ask your advice when he's taking out your appendix. So there are some things that we've just got to get onto; we can't wait.' It is fair enough, but nevertheless, moving amongst blacks, you get the continuing feeling of remoteness, of still 'being done to'. It might, in time, prove to be necessary, regardless of whatever practical difficulties may crop up, to give a sense of participation to a few blacks other than those same, predictable faces.

The 'well, you can't do much with them, can you?' attitude that Bryant spoke about is the attitude that Professor Colin Tatz highlighted so well in his 'The Politics of Aboriginal Health'. Field staff and bureaucrats tend to take the view that 'the Aboriginal problem is really no one's fault because there are cultural barriers not susceptible of penetration'. Even though adverse conditions in black health, housing, employment, education, etc. etc. *do* exist, and *could* be eradicated by adequate financing and management; somehow it is *black* hopelessness, *black* obstinacy, that is at fault, not the overt racist assumptions of a white bureaucracy that either prevents the actual help being given, or else ensures that it is given in such a way as to be useless for black purposes. The attitude of some of the white welfare officers and staff in places like Hooker Creek (Northern Territory) have been described to me as something quite appalling, by people who have been up there. As Sister Helen Wagner put it after her resignation from the Northern Territory Welfare Board late in 1971:

> As an Australian nurse I deplore the attitude that the Aborigines are so dirty that a few more germs make no difference. As a Christian I deplore the double moral standard which underlies the disregard for the sacredness of life.

Knowing quite well that the general attitude of the welfare staff in way out places is no secret, Gordon Bryant was asked at Newcastle whether he didn't agree that for any real change to come about, three quarters of the entrenched welfare staff would have to be phased out. Said he:

> No. As a friendly socialist character, I don't feel like kicking anybody around. People might feel that the new climate is inhospitable to them and they might apply for a job elsewhere. But in the interviews I've had with these people, I found that when I set out what the objectives were and how it was to be proceeded with, I think they caught on. It's going to take a while for it to seep through

> and there's only one of me and although my senior staff like Mr Dexter and Ray McKenzie and so on can do something, I've got more facilities for moving around and sort of thumping the table and demanding that they be more consultative and less dictatorial and a bit more dynamic, I might say. I think the structure has got to be changed rather than the people. People might be taken out and given new postings and so on ...

Apparently the new atmosphere did sweep through the welfare ranks pretty quickly, for a press release on March 29 reported that Mr Bryant endorsed the recommendations made by a seminar held at Batchelor to examine Aboriginal development in the Northern Territory. The seminar had been arranged by the Department of Aboriginal Affairs and attended by representatives from it, other government departments, mission authorities, managers of Aboriginal progress associations and so forth. All agreed that the overriding principle of government policy should be one of community self-determination for blacks. Further,

> the seminar had concluded that communities must have a measure of freedom in the use of resources provided by the government and some tolerance of what might be conventionally regarded as wastage would be necessary to allow responsibility to develop. There should therefore be provision for the involvement of the community in the executive processes where services and resources were provided by government and other organisations at the request of the community. This would necessitate direct access by the community to the area where decisions are made.

It's great stuff and if it gets to be even half true what an achievement it will be. However, to get it even half true will require a tolerance of Aboriginal attitudes and a level of meaningful consultation that hasn't yet been exhibited by the gubbah anywhere. Can you really see them stopping calling the tune anywhere? See them having the imagination to really leave it to blacks to work out? But more on that theme later.

Of course Gordon Bryant is in the position of having to straddle two alien cultures with largely conflicting aims and values. Also he *is* a friendly socialist character. And he is a politician. Even if he *were* more willing to get tough on blacks' behalf and get whites off their backs, the incontrovertible fact is that, however sympathetic, he is a white man in a white government, elected by a white majority. That is what Gerry Bostock meant when he said: 'I don't believe there'll be any major changes with this bloody new government, because they're mainly concerned with their white supporters not a one per cent minority.' Of course there *have* been changes and there will, I believe, be more. But to what meaningful degree? Because the continuing crunch, apart from white racism, is LAND. I wonder whether, in the south, any government will ever have the strength or the imagination to push the land issue to a real point of justice.

At its second meeting in Canberra early in May, the Interim Consultative Committee called for Mr Justice Woodward to be removed from the federal government's enquiry into land rights and replaced by six Aboriginals who would have the right to appoint qualified advisers on legal and other matters. The government's response was to widen the terms of reference of the Woodward Commission on land rights to include the states as well as the Northern Territory, so illustrating that 'meaningful consultation' is one thing and the crunch is another.

And of course land for southern blacks is going to be the tough one. In the more remote areas you only have to buy land off one station owner, or do a deal with one mining company. But in the south, wherever you go, land that was black land, reserve land, in the memory of middle-aged Aborigines, had by 1973 been gradually filched off them piece by piece. Just about every Aboriginal reserve used to be a lot larger than it is now but has been whittled down by local graziers with influence in the right places, whether by lease or by purchase, I don't know. 'We used to camp over there when I was a kid, but they moved us off, over to here', is a common tale. This land isn't going to be got back so easily. A black passing through here a couple of days ago told me that an official in Moree is sitting on a good slice of black land out there. I don't know whether it is true, but if it is, how do blacks get redress? It's one thing to move blacks off, holus-bolus, when it suits anyone, but can you imagine the concerted 'security of tenure' squeal that would go up if anyone tried to even suggest that, in all fairness, it should happen to a white man?

The minister stressed several times that the government didn't want to dispossess anyone. Yet for land justice for blacks to even begin to be arrived at, this may at times be necessary. Frank Roberts' old Land Board had records of dozens of large tracts of Aboriginal land that had been alienated. Imagine that a grazier has built a $30,000 home on what was, not long ago, black land. And I don't just mean 'all of Australia' type black land, but identifiable areas that were either actual reserves or places of long habitual black use. He might have a clear title to it, but say blacks claim it by virtue of wrongful alienation in the not too distant past. What would happen next? The Country Party had one answer: 'Ignore the blacks. If necessary, strong-arm them.' But this has gone out of fashion. So what, indeed, happens next? Said Frank Roberts:

> I just don't know what measures would have to be adopted. There would have to be government intervention. Just what the Aboriginal people would do in a situation like that, I don't know. Such a house would put a different aspect on it. It is difficult to say just what would happen. It would need much negotiation.

Negotiation, yes — and compromise. In some of the cases — and in many, the facts are a lot stranger than the fiction — the government must have the power of resumption, as they have for every piddling development scheme dreamt up by bureaucrats. In other cases, perhaps justice can be achieved by giving blacks, after due consultation, alternative land and compensation. Whatever happens, I cannot see that the $5 million a year for the next ten years that has been allocated for land purchase for blacks will be adequate, or even near adequate.

To give some idea of what it's like from a black point of view and to give some idea of the difficulties that land for southern blacks is going to pose, the following example is useful. At Newcastle, Mick Saunders, one of the blacks from Purfleet, asked the minister about land rights for Purfleet Reserve, which is about three miles south of Taree (New South Wales), on the Pacific Highway. The ensuing dialogue had touches of pure comedy, yet the issues raised are less funny. Answering Mick's question about land rights for Purfleet, Gordon Bryant said:

> The question of how this will be decided is still before the … Now what you should do, I'm serious about this, you people on the ground have got to go out to work out what you reckon is your tribal ground and submit that to Judge Woodward. Draw a sketch of it. I can't give you an undertaking that we'll buy it all back for you or anything like that — but that's the way I feel about it.
>
> [Emotion had got the best of Mick and he had interjected at several points during the above answer. Then:]
>
> *Mick*: Why should it be bought back if we owned it in the first place?
>
> *Minister*: I don't know, except that if there was some person living on it, with a house and everything else, we're not going to deprive him of land rights to give it to somebody else … to help them by damaging the first one …
>
> *Mick*: There's nobody on it …
>
> *Minister*: Well, if there's nobody on it …
>
> *Mick*: Why can't you give it to us now?
>
> *Minister*: I'm telling you what to do! Write out, draw a little sketch, set it out on paper, post it to us to hand on to Judge Woodward …

Mick: mutter, mutter, mutter …

Minister: I'm quite serious about this. It's no good, for the Aboriginal people or anybody else, to ask for a say in their own affairs and then expect somebody else to go and do a simple job like that. Now there's plenty of people on Purfleet who could get to work and produce something like that. Now you've got to do it!

Mick: Excuse me! We've also got a main highway running right through the middle … a main highway that's been put through the middle of our land … where it didn't go in the first place! It used to go around through Gloucester way. We've had about five children hit. And now it's coming up very shortly, they're working on it now … they're going to put a four lane highway, a widening, right through the middle of us!

Minister: Well, you've got to try and stop that by getting onto local council and your local state member and so on …

Mick: They take no notice of us!

Minister: Have you been to see them lately? What's his name? …

Mick: They're a little bit too busy to see us …

Minister: They *aren't* too busy to see you! Look, if I'm not too busy to come here tonight …

Mick: Yeah, *but they are up there*!

Minister: Well, when you've been to see them, and they've told you that they're too busy to see you, you write to me and I'll get on his wheel!

Mick: They wouldn't even put the pedestrian crossing up only we — the little few people here now — got them to put them up … and lights, too. That's why people got run over …

Minister: We'll have to stop now, but you're in the same boat as everybody else. Councils, municipal governments, state governments, federal governments — they all do the same. You've got to kick against them!

Mick: That's why we've come here asking you and the rest of your staff to do something about it!

[At this stage a white interjector called on the chairman to end the questioning. Perhaps he didn't like to see Jacky having *too* much say in his own affairs. The minister reassuringly said 'We'll do our best' as Mick, still trying, began to ask:]

Mick: What about this motel they're building on our land just down the road from my house?

That finished the dialogue. From the minister's speech, the blacks naturally thought that justice had come. So, they got straight to the nitty-gritty only to find that Santa Claus isn't for real and the Year of Jubilo doesn't really ever arrive. Perhaps in terms of human evolution, if not human justice, this is just as well. All the same, is it any wonder that blacks continue to feel that white Australia has 'em by the short hairs?

6

An Act of Faith

> I feel that things like massive medical aid, educational aid, legal aid and so on are all only a bandage on the real problem facing this country — racism. I can't see the real problem as being anything else. The white superiority thing in this country — and not just this country but all over the world where white groups dominate — is the problem. For some reason they seem to think that they are superior. I know that I've had it drummed into me — all my life! Racism, classism, sexism — it's all linked. The boss kicks the white man. He kicks the black man. The black man kicks the black woman and the black woman neglects the black kids. So the whole education of people, and I don't just mean formal education, the whole living structure of people has to change.
>
> *Kaye Bellear*

Between them, Kaye and Bob Bellear have probably done more than anybody else to turn the Redfern Community Housing Project into a reality — with the behind-the-scenes backing of the Rev Ted Kennedy of the St Vincent's Roman Catholic Presbytery at Redfern — a man who, in my estimation, is one of the few who gives real substance to his profession of Christian love. Kaye and Bob are members of the Redfern Aboriginal Housing Committee, a group that had been formed to do something about the homeless blacks in the area, discrimination against Aborigines by landlords and rent extortion. Said Bob Bellear in March after the Federal Labor Government had been in for a little over three months:

> We want to purchase a block of land in Redfern. It is bounded by Eveleigh, Louis, Vine and Caroline Streets. The project contains sixty-eight houses, and two factories and in this we hope to renovate and build the houses and shorten all backyards so as to make a communal yard in the middle. We want to have a child-minding centre, an Aboriginal Family Education Centre, at one end and a community hall at the other end and house a lot of the Aborigines in Redfern who are being pushed out by the white developers. It's not going to be a free rental system though — most people are sick of the handout system — but we've got to work out the details yet through negotiation with the government. And it won't be a ghetto either — at least any more than Redfern is already. There's one or two houses in the block which whites still occupy. They are prepared to live in the same area with Aborigines and go along with the project. And by all means they can stay. They're welcome.
>
> Our project certainly brought the racists out of the South Sydney Council's woodwork. They're only dead set on getting the blacks out of the inner city area and into Mt Druitt. Kaye rang up Jim Cope, who is the ALP member for the Redfern area and also the government speaker and asked him what he could do about the homeless blacks in Redfern. He said if there were homeless blacks in the Northern Territory or the Australian Capital Territory he could do something. But homeless blacks in his own electorate weren't of his concern. And those were his exact words. Because we felt that there would be a lot of cooperation between the South Sydney Council and the state government over the housing project, we by-passed them and went straight to the Labor government

in Canberra. Could you imagine us being so stupid as to let Waddy [New South Wales Minister in charge of Aboriginal affairs] get a sniff of it beforehand?

In April, Aboriginal Affairs Minister Bryant announced that the federal government would back the project to the tune of $530,000. As a result, Jim Cope, New South Wales Labor leader Pat Hills and the Mayor of South Sydney, Ald Bill Hartup teamed up to persuade him of the error of the decision. There hadn't been consultation; did the government realise that the project envisaged a centre for alcoholics at one end and a pre-school at the other; what about the threat of a potential ghetto implicit with threats of race wars etc.?

Redfern residents put it rather more crudely. Said one of the people who signed a protest petition against the new project: 'Fancy encouraging the bloody boongs to come here. There's too many here already. Why not keep them out in the country where they belong?' Another protester, interestingly enough part-Aboriginal herself, explained her opposition in terms of, 'We're a different class of people to that lot.' She had, she said, 'fought all my life to be a lady' and didn't see why these blacks should get what she saw as preferential treatment. (It is interesting to see how a certain type of Koori seems to absorb to its very marrow the essence of white middle class values and respectability in psychological reaction against their own beginnings and so become, as it were, whiter than white.) Anyhow, what the petitioners, combined, were up in arms against were allegations that the housing project would quickly degenerate into a ghetto of no-hopers, alcoholics, prostitutes and brawlers. Some had, they said, taken to carrying knives in self-defence against the street violence that had already occurred in the area. The prevailing point of view was put rather well in the feature 'Conservative Comment' by 'Libertas', published one feels against the grain but in the interests of balanced content by *Nation Review* (19–27/4/73)

When you dislike a man who is black, that does not make you a racist. You are a racist only if you dislike him *because* he is black. This is a simple truth and yet I will venture to assert that much of what small 'l' liberals today call 'racism' falls into the first rather than into the latter category. Take this affair recently headlined as RACISM IN REDFERN. Several hundred white residents petitioned the local council to bar the takeover of several terrace houses in their area for the purpose of setting up an 'aboriginal community'. Does this mean American-style colour prejudice has come to Australia? Sydney TV showed that there were indeed violent emotions involved — with an actual confrontation between a white protester and a black organiser being shown. The grounds for protest were informative, however. Aboriginals were in fact already squatting in many of these terrace houses and the local residents had come to find them singularly unpleasant neighbours — drunken shouting, fighting and bottle smashing at all hours of almost every night, aboriginals urinating in the street and shouting obscenities at passing white housewives. Who would not want to see the last of neighbours such as that — whether they were black, white or had purple polka dots? It is in fact a most violent denial of civil rights if we stigmatise people who protest against such things as 'racists' — just because the offensive group is identifiable in terms of colour. Black is *not* beautiful — any more than white is. The greatest obstacle to a reasoned discussion of white 'backlash' is an unstated assumption by many of Australia's suburbanites that aboriginals are just the same as they are except that they have a brown skin. It is this assumption that makes what anti-aboriginal protesters say seem so unintelligible and unreasonable. 'I wouldn't like someone to object to me just because I had a brown skin,' the suburbanite says. Of course the anti-aboriginal protester is *not* just objecting to skin colour. He could scarcely be so puerile. He objects to what does factually go with skin colour — habits, behaviour and practices that white society has long preached against and condemns. If it were just the colour of their skin that set aboriginals apart, there would be no backlash. It is then this fact that aboriginals are characterised by behaviour that in a white we would find despicable that suburban small 'l' liberals find so hard to absorb. I know of several instances where such liberals, when actually meeting aboriginals for the first time, have suddenly become much more conservative in their views. It is well known that it is in country towns and depressed urban areas that anti-aboriginal feeling runs high. What people from both types of areas have in common is that they have actually met and lived near aboriginals. They know what they are talking about. Obviously there is no necessary assumption that these differences between aboriginals and whites are inborn. All of them could be attributed to differences in upbringing. We come from a culture that values privacy, hygiene and industriousness. Aboriginals do not. We see the virtue of competition and emotional reserve. Aboriginals do not.

White backlash is then reasonable. Unless we expect whites to forget overnight the cultural values that they have learned and practised all their lives, they will find the proximity of aboriginals unpleasant.

There are three possible solutions to this problem: change the whites; change the aboriginals; or have the two groups live apart. The first two solutions seem totally presumptuous and paternalistic — if not fascist. The last is the solution that has usually emerged. Blacks and whites, if left to themselves, normally do live in separate communities. It is only when governments and white do-gooders interfere with the natural selection processes that problems arise.

When two white people have a fight, passers-by shrug and go on their way. When two blacks fight, they shrug and say 'bloody Abos — always fighting'. When a black man and a white man have a fight they call it a race-war and ring the newspapers. It is the *interaction* that causes the publicity. Instances of drinking, bad behaviour and so forth during the early period when the Aboriginal Housing Committee had not yet organised itself into imposing its own restraints in the form of nightly patrols by ex-boxer Dick Blair, were enough to cause the anti-black reaction amongst residents. Would a students' commune, behaving in much the same way have caused as quick and as vehement a reaction? And *do* all blacks in Redfern urinate in the street? Why did we hear nothing of it until the housing project was announced?

It is true enough that black control by blacks is an important factor needed in the housing project. Any of the chaotic reserves testify to that. But does that mean that the chance for blacks to prove that they can control the more unruly elements amongst themselves should be denied them? The oft-cited case of the slum clearance project in London in the '30s is a case in point. The slums were replaced by new flats. Within months, goes the story, they were wrecked — bathtubs full of coal, windows broken and so forth. What happened afterwards? Are these people or their children still smashing flats? If so, is it because that line of behaviour demonstrably goes along with their skin colour? Or have these people, given decent housing, *gradually adapted* themselves so as to be less of a problem? Isn't this, roughly speaking, how the process of social change, of growth, would be achieved?

Does any line of behaviour factually go with skin colour? Or is it rather a fact that skin colour keeps people tied within an environment that produces riotous behaviour and contempt/hatred for the white man's laws? Remember that it is commonly acknowledged on Aboriginal reserves that the darker children get the worst go at school. Blackness is the real liability. People of this colour have been put into the position they are in today. Skin colour alone is a potent creator of the aversion-suspicion reaction in whites. Recently a mechanic did a job on my car. The bill was $70. I told him that I would pay within ten days. He started sweating about it and his attitude showed me that, on the basis of my skin colour, he deduced that I wouldn't pay, even though I have dealt with him for a long time. Had a white man told him the same thing then he would have accepted it — without any actual reason for being able to trust him. Don't tell me that black skin doesn't make a difference.

On the subject of the anti-black feelings of those who have lived near Aborigines: examples of black degeneracy and white reaction to it are frequent enough, Aborigines are a broken race. In their modern manifestation, they are indeed pathetic by-products of colonisation. Yet despite their appalling history, it is amazing how many black families have managed to get themselves out of the psychological bind that afflicts so many blacks. They have done so often in the face of considerable resistance from white people. They are now enjoying an equal standard of living and many have managed to do so without feeling the need to deny their racial origins. Those who have not yet managed to get out are Australia's historical chickens come home to roost. White society created them; often fathered them. Now it is stuck with them. Unless it can find ways to begin to help them to help themselves — for nothing else will work — the conditions and psychological context that has created the type of blacks that 'Libertas' complains about will be perpetuated. And, it must be recorded in passing, blacks who have lived in Housing Commission estates in various areas haven't exactly been rapt in admiration of their white neighbours either. The subtlety of the tricks and twists of the human mind, whether expressed by a white person or a black person, goes rather beyond the generalities of description of a 'Libertas'. The fine truth is always more subtle.

What does, factually, go with black skin? Obviously not, in that writer's view, a regard for privacy, hygiene and industriousness. Privacy is a virtue more easily achieved if there are not say, three bedrooms, parents and eleven children in a house. How can blacks value something that many have never experienced? Hygiene is quite an achievement when, as at so many Aboriginal reserves, there is no hot or cold running water, no adequate toilet facilities, no adequate drainage, etc. Hygiene is a matter of what you are used to. When I was in prison I worked for a while as a clerk in the reception room. One of my duties was to get whites remanded for sentence out of their civilian clothes and into prison uniforms. I often had reason to gag at the filthy state and smell of their underwear. Quite a few of these men had to be made to wash and clean their teeth, not only at first, but right through their stay. Hygiene is *not* the preserve of a particular skin colour.

Re the third point. Industriousness is usually a function of motivation. Blacks are rarely given adequate motivation to want to work for long periods. Usually they are not on equal pay in the first place. Even if they are paid fairly, they will often work only to the point where they feel that they have enough money. After that their value system says 'stop' — and their value system is their own business, and their own cultural right. If blacks were working for themselves instead of for a white man's benefit, they would probably do twice as much before calling a halt. It is a function of motivation. How many white men will slog unceasingly for a poor wage or a hard boss? But they will when they are their own boss, and when they get the benefit of their own labour. It is the adequate motivation of blacks that I see as the central problem and challenge confronting those who would seek to do something about the 'Aboriginal problem'.

Regarding separate communities. These are precisely what the reserves have always been. It is what apartheid is all about. Separate communities are one thing if they are imposed on blacks and enforced by the white race for its own economic gain as in South Africa. They are quite another if they are *chosen* by blacks and established on black terms. There is obviously a world of difference between the two — human coercion and disadvantage as against human choice and human dignity. It is a subject discussed more fully in a later chapter. 'Libertas' says that, 'blacks and whites, if left to themselves, normally do live in separate communities' — which solution, the context suggests, he supports. As Bobbi Sykes would say, agreeing fully with this point of view: '*I'm* not stopping him from going back to his own white country! Certainly, let him go and leave Australia as it has been for thousands of years — a contented, separate, all-black country.' See? No disagreement at all.

But of course, it just isn't so easy any more. The point, surely, of giving the housing project the green light was to give blacks a chance to prove that a black-planned, black-run, black-directed venture can work. A 'yes it's very good but' letter to *The Daily Telegraph* (7/5/73) pointed out that however well-intentioned the plan, one cannot change human nature and habits in a crash programme. Stated the letter:

> People, who, through economic hardship, social neglect and inadequate education have grown up in appalling surroundings cannot be changed overnight into responsible householders.

In fact I know of cases where black women who had lived all of their lives in shacks with dirt floors, given a decent home, have been so pleased and proud that the home is kept spotless. I also know of cases where the reverse is true — cases where blacks wreck their new home and neglect it. Is either case anything to generalise from? If it were shown that sixty per cent of all lower middle class students fail their first year at university, is that a reason to bar all lower middle class students?

Dick Blair said that the government's grant was 'the first chance we've had in 200 years'. Because there is no need for white professionals constantly to be at the pivot of the housing project as they must be in the Legal Service and the Medical Service, it can be a far more autonomous black concern. In this lies its challenge to the Redfern black community. The blacks have got to show the white community that faith in blacks' ability can be justified. God knows, they'll be watching like hawks. And I don't doubt that an element will be doing their best to foment trouble and test black authority on the site. The blacks have got to show that they can impose discipline amongst their own. Here is the crunch, for Redfern's young radicals, having only so recently taken the bit between their teeth, don't like the sound of discipline. Imagine how some of them are going to take to being forcibly ejected for drunken, disorderly behaviour in Caroline St. Already this element has plenty of jibes about Dick Blair's patrol methods. But blacks are going to have to learn that you can't have your cake and eat it too. Without internal discipline, the movement will never really get out to where it is really needed — the Aboriginal reserves.

It seems to me that the Redfern (actually Chippendale) project can develop in either of two ways. It can gradually weed out all the families that do not toe a predetermined line and thus become a type of better blacks' residential. Alternatively, it can develop into a true social experiment, a commune incorporating both traditional Aboriginal life styles and European ideas into a synthesis that has meaning for both races. It can become a place that lifts the horizons of all blacks who go there. It can become a place that racists can't deride. When I consider who is running the project, and then compare this with who *could* have been running it, then I do think that it has a very good chance of being a success.

There are hundreds of homeless blacks in the inner city area. Right at the bottom of the pile are the 'goomies'. These are the Aboriginal alcoholics, the metho drinkers, who probably have the lowest status of any human being in this country. A section of the housing project is reserved for them. White alcoholics, equally on skid row, are also welcome. Say the Bellears:

> Everyone could learn a lesson in integration — in how people *can* live together with colour not entering into it one bit — from the goomies. They are the only ones we've seen, who can live together without colour even being thought of. They accept the humanity in any other goom, whether he's black or white. We don't believe that most of the goomies will ever stop drinking. All we can do is give them somewhere to belong, give them vitamin tablets, meals and fix up their cuts and bruises and make their dying a little less painful. To be perfectly honest, we can't see anybody really giving a stuff. There should be programmes instituted to stop fifteen year olds getting on the metho. To stop twenty year olds getting on the metho. But when you get to the stage of being thirty-five or forty

and you've been on it for ten years ... Sure, we often wonder what the hell we're wasting our time for. You make a goomie feel better and off he goes for another drink. But at least he isn't in the bloody agony that you often see these people in. And it's not a self-inflicted agony in many cases. Not like most white alcoholics. That's the difference that racism makes. It's because a lot of them have never been *allowed* to do the sorts of things that whites take for granted. They haven't had equal opportunities as far as housing is concerned, as far as employment is concerned, as far as education is concerned. They're been brought up on this filthy flour, sugar 'n tea diet. They've taken all the bad things out of the white man's diet and kept none of the valuable eating habits of the old people. How can you keep kids clean if you haven't got any water? People say soap is cheap. Soap is *not* cheap — it's bloody dear — about 30c a cake. Bread comes before soap and, often, grog comes before bread. Because people get *so* bloody desperate and they've been so bloody desperate for 150 years. For many, grog is habitual. Their parents did it. Their grandparents did it. What's the point of eating properly anyway? Because it doesn't matter whether you eat properly or not — you're still going to get kicked in the guts. A lot of the gooms can only be themselves when they're drunk. It's the only time that they feel a sense of security. So, for them, grog's just a massive escape. It *is* the major health problem. And behind it, in turn, is the racial problem.

The racial problem. I do not think that many whites in this country realise how much black people hate them, collectively, for what has been done to the Aboriginal race. When Alice Briggs (in Chapter 1) said, 'I don't really hate white people ...' she may have believed it, but her day-to-day attitudes show differently. The hatred is never very far from the surface and her daily experiences never give her any reason to alter. The majority of young, and not so young radicals are the same. Charles Perkins warns:

> Some of the whites who have come into Aboriginal affairs of late — people of a good heart, good types with a good motivation — are the ones who are going to get hurt, unfortunately. While the people who have done the most damage in Aboriginal affairs over the past twenty or thirty years or before that even, are just going to get off scot free. It's the new ones that are going to get hurt.

Kaye Bellear does get hurt. She says that the degree of open anti-white racism from the Redfern blacks has intensified in the last twelve months and she feels it pretty deeply at times.

> It's time a lot of them started to direct their anti-white feelings in a direction that was effective — at the real enemies, for Christ's sake! Because I'm not their enemy! They should start directing it at those who are really kicking them in the guts! But I don't think they know who that is, anyway. And that isn't their fault, either. As they start to establish themselves, these blacks are going to become more and more racist — until they finally get to the point where they'll equal out …

There is an interesting inevitability about all of this. As Bobbi Sykes reminds us:

> I think that in the words of a very great African man, the whole thing can be summed up whichever way things go. This African man said, 'When you took your foot off the neck of the black man, did you expect him to look up and smile with gratitude?' I think that you could say the same thing about the situation in Australia. Does anyone seriously expect the blacks to fawn with gratitude, to lick boots for small favours which are 200 years late?

7

Call to Violence

TONY (THE SEEDING ...)

I remember Mumma — when the baby came along
We were livin' at the old Trelawney place
And we couldn't get a doctor he was much too far away
And we hadn't any money so he wouldn't treat OUR race
Daddy lived on station handouts for the bit of work he did
And we ate off the wild rabbits that he caught
Or when we were real hungry he would go and steal a sheep
He'd laugh and bring it in the door 'Look what I've bought!'
But the laughter slowly faded as my mumma's time drew near
Her body hunchin' tightly up with pain
The crinkle lines upon his face grew deep and dark with fear
As he rode out for the doctor who would not come, again.

I remember Mumma when the baby came along
With her hands screwed tight around the old bedstead

Her dear, dear body twitching, screaming all that awful night
Till silence came with morning — both were dead.
Now we live back on the mission and my daddy is a drunk
It's not as nice as old Trelawney place
I'm gonna be a doctor when I grow up some day
Or a soldier — captain maybe and I'll fight for my black race!

Yeah, I'll fight 'em on my own some day so no one else gits hurt
And I'll shoot their soldiers — every bloody man
Until they know the wrong they do and why my mumma died
Yeah, one day I'm gonna shoot right back —
I'LL MAKE them understand!!

THE FLOWERING ...

When the white man took his bloodied boot
From the neck of the buggared black
Did you expect some gratitude
His smile 'Good on you Jack?'
When your psalmist sang
Of a suffering Christ
While you practised genocide
Did you expect his hate would fade
Out of sight with the ebbing tide?
In another time, another age
If fate had reversed the play
And a hard black boot pressed on your white throat
When released — what would you say
Friends and pals forever together in a new fair dawn
Or meet like you and I shall meet
With flames and with daggers drawn.

The 1967 Referendum gave a huge 'yes' vote for full citizenship rights for Aborigines. Many blacks thought that at last a new deal for black people was imminent. The disillusionment after 1967 hit hard. It is little wonder that younger, more literate blacks began to search for their values in the literature of the Black Panther movement of the United States. They read somewhere about how some white fat cat reckoned that Australia was a 'lucky country' and said 'Yeah, for the gubbahs'. Once again they are told of a case of rape of a black girl and hear the oft told tale that the coppers regard sex offences against blacks *with great tolerance.* If blacks get drunk, they get busted and cop-bullied not because they are drunk so much, but because they're *black* and drunk. I mean it — just ask yourselves whether you ever see the cops waiting to catch 'em reeling out of the RSL at night. It would be more than a cop would dare. The young blacks remember how the white kids sniggered at them in high school. (That's what made them leave — despite all the good offices of the Secondary Schools Grant.) They've probably heard the president of the Aboriginal Advancement Association back on the reserve trying to make himself and his listeners believe that, 'If we just wait a bit longer, the whites *will* help us, things *will* get better.' They've probably walked out of the meeting to go and get drunk. There's some reality in that. So they come to the city and some black shows them what Malcolm X, an American black, said:

> So don't you run around trying to make friends with somebody who's depriving you of your rights. They're not your friends, no, they're your enemies. Treat them like that and fight them, and you'll get freedom; and after you get your freedom, your enemy will respect you.

They read it and it figures, it makes sense.

Or perhaps they read Frederick Douglass:

> The limits of tyrants are prescribed by the endurance of those whom they oppress. [And] If there is no struggle,

> there is no progress. Those who profess to favour freedom, and yet depreciate agitation, are men who want crops without ploughing up the ground. They want rain without thunder and lightning. They want the ocean without the awful roar of its many waters.

And that makes sense too.

Many country Aborigines are afraid of 'Black Power' because to them it has meant urban Aborigines descending on their town, kicking up hell about something, usually pub or wage discrimination, and clearing out. The local blacks are left, undefended, to cop the inevitable white reprisals. Nevertheless, the idea of Black Power has enabled many Aborigines, especially the younger generation, to lift their heads towards a vision of hope and a new dignity. It has brought a subtle change to many of the most down-trodden, frightened communities and it is no accident that all blacks who knew of the Embassy and understood its aims, hailed its message — land rights for black Australia. Concurrent with this is the fact that blacks everywhere are no longer just accepting but are volubly questioning the squalor, the purposelessness, the waste of their lives and the social condition they find themselves in.

Black Power, as symbol, signifies the return to pride, to manhood, for Aborigines who have long ago lost the status of men. It will provide a new identity-image, this time positive. It will, in time, spell the end of the drunken 'give us two bob mate' cur who slinks up to you in a country town. It will provide an avenue of expression. Black Power is a very new concept in this country and, unlike its American counterpart, has produced little real violence to date. The violent scenes that were a feature when the Embassy was ripped down were, all participants and spectators agree, police initiated, with the blacks only defending themselves and their tent.

Expressed positively, Black Power means black men and black women speaking out and uniting to force the white man to acknowledge their humanity, rights, justice, dignity and right to self-determination. It is the voice of a dispossessed, victimised minority making a fair, human claim. Expressed negatively, it becomes disillusionment and frustration which is expressed not by alcoholic self-destruction as in the past, but by violence against the white persecutors. I asked Charles Perkins how things would develop if tribal and urban blacks were once again short-changed after a period of hope, as happened after 1967. Would there be violence? Said he:

> Some groups probably will [turn to it]. It must be part and parcel of their development if frustration continues. Violence will be part and parcel of Aboriginal affairs in the future. It just can't be any other way. It will probably happen anyway, regardless of what good measures are going to be implemented by the Labor government. It is going to happen in some areas, as a spontaneous thing. It has happened in the last two or three years quite dramatically on lots of missions and reserves. A can has been put on this, to keep it quiet. Nobody knows about it at all. Yet it has happened frequently. It has to be expected because the people have been suppressed for so long and they're just sick and tired of promises, programmes, pilot projects and being told what to do by the white bosses and administrators. Having things planned for them by people who don't really have their interest at heart. Being deceived and denied things. I think they are just going to hit out.

As I attended meetings and asked questions both of city and outback blacks, the idea of impending violence came through repeatedly both from the articulate blacks and from those whose depth of pain and hatred had left them almost incoherent on the subject. And over and over again they stressed that violence is necessary, not as aggression so much (although that is part of it) as for *defence*, defence against police persecution and acts of small-town and city bullying by whites. As Paul Coe put it:

> I don't believe any Aboriginal will initiate violence. But I believe that, like all groups around the world who have

> been colonised, Aborigines will take a defensive role. They will ensure that they survive as a race. They will ensure that their kids don't keep dying from malnutrition, that they will not be used and abused as cheap labour. I think that when you take into account the institutionalised violence that most Aborigines have to live under and their psychic reactions against it, then you've got to find a way, some kind of defensive mechanism that allows the people to survive as a race and I think that one day, the outgrowth of this, of Aboriginal men and women picking up guns, will be just. To me, the idea that the Aboriginal people will one day pick up the gun, to use it perhaps, to build their own separate state or find some other way of ensuring that the race *does* survive, is a just one. It's something that I'm not frightened of because it is something that's just got to happen. I see that there will be no alternative ...

Even the more conservative elements agree on this. Neville Bonner stated, after the fall of the Embassy, a peaceful black demonstration, 'I can't see how violence can be avoided now.' Pastor Frank Roberts commented,

> The militants have become a creative force — creative for the betterment of the Aboriginal people in their own way. There is definitely a place for militancy. We cannot remain docile too much longer ... we *must* assert ourselves. I think that if this government fails the Aboriginal people now, if it falls down on its promises and betrays the Aborigines it will be a bad day for the Australian people.

On the face of it, Aboriginal violence against white Australia is somewhat like a gnat challenging an elephant. Blacks in this country are historically a non-violent, peaceable people. The white race has always been keen to turn to violence, especially if it is against blacks, so they wouldn't take much provoking to turn on the big guns against a troublesome black minority. Such were the considerations of ex-army man Gerry Bostock when he said, apropos black violence:

> If violence erupts, the blacks will be annihilated because they haven't got the manpower or the financial resources ... There *will* be violence, but the blacks will lose in the end.

Perhaps there will be a new black soon. A black, who, completely alienated, will consider that to lose in the end is not too great a price to pay to re-purchase the manhood of the Aboriginal race. Figure it out. How many white men would stand by and watch their children dying from starvation and neglect? Watch them being oppressed and stigmatised? Watch them being crippled? Perhaps the cost will be some black martyrs. And they won't come from the ranks of the fashionably dressed, TV pomaded, Afro-frizzed public blacks. It is a different black that I have in mind. You see them at black meetings. They never speak up. They never draw attention to themselves. They get a bit bored with the rhetoric of Black Power, because, essentially, they are doers, not talkers. They only perk up when someone suggests a line of action, because this has real meaning. So, when someone suggests that it's time for a demo outside Parliament House in Sydney, or perhaps we should storm Pinchgut or, let's go and camp on Waddy's lawn, it's 'Yeah, let's go.' There is no fear. They are ready for action and only need good leadership to become an effective kamikaze force. Ten years ago their type all became hopeless reserve drunks. Today they don't, for now they have been given a purpose. I believe it is these blacks who will achieve a return to manhood for Aboriginal men.

There are dreams about ... vague plans of how blacks could form guerilla bands. Get a few with the bushmanship of a Lionel Brockman and you'd have quite an effective force provided you could get the thing financed by outside sympathisers. In the USA, whenever white society does another rotten thing to blacks, black resentment expresses itself in terms of dragging whites out of cars and giving them a hiding, or summer ghetto riots, or by firing a building full of white tenants. That, say Aborigines with whom I have discussed these things, is maybe OK if you number 22 million. But when you are as tiny a minority as blacks in this country, you have to act less on emotion and more with the intellect. Say a black girl is forced into sex with some coppers in South Australia. It's no good, obviously, complaining to the cops. And of course, the same cops have got tabs on all the local blacks. But if these blacks could alert a central group which could organise for a punitive group from another state to move in to take the justice denied to them by the white system and then move out of the region just as quickly, it would be quite a different thing. It would not be difficult to enforce secrecy amongst blacks and, were a type of 'cell' system used, working through a central group, any leaks that did occur could be quickly pin-pointed and sealed without undue fuss. Provided adequate organisation was kept, only a handful of people in each state would be needed to form a guerilla force against white violence.

Some blacks stress that there is no sense in having blind-rage reprisals against white people whose only crime is that they happen to have been born with a white skin. They stress that a guerilla system would eliminate much of the injustice to innocent by-standers, both white and black, that characterises the Black Power uprisings of the USA. There is no profit either in hurting innocent whites to whom no personal blame for the state blacks are in can be attached and who might very well support the Aboriginal cause. Similarly, there is no profit in needlessly causing a white reaction on a scale which would turn into a race war. However there *is* profit in the concept of fast moving reprisal units that can sink out of sight into any black population after bringing a measure of justice to a preselected figure who has a record of racist bullying in any area.

Of course blacks realise that with conditions as they are today, there is still a large element of romance in these ideas. Probably Aboriginals will have to wait at least one, if not more generations before they can fund and organise themselves to this extent. And, some blacks argue, the best action is not against the white man's person, but against his property, for property is his god. Reprisals against white injustice would, in this view, be better directed against petrol, electricity or gas installations. Against dams, bridges, railways and aerodromes. Against foreign-owned ships, to get a focus of international publicity. Or mass poisoning of the waterholes of stud stock could be thought about. Wheat fields and forests could be razed, using chemical substances that ignite after a delay.

That blacks have got to the point of dreaming such dreams is in itself an indictment of Australia's treatment of its black people. It is incredible, considering Australia's affluence, that a peaceful race of people should be forced to fight to attain justice in the land of their fathers.

It may, in time, be proven that it is necessary to do this. We should remember the words of that great patriot Mahatma Gandhi in answer to a question on the use of violence in the defence of rights (published in *The Guardian,* 16/12/38):

> Where the choice is set between cowardice and violence I would advise violence. I praise and extol the serene courage of dying without killing. Yet I desire that those who have not this courage should rather cultivate the art of killing and being killed, than basely to avoid the danger. This is because he who runs away commits mental violence; he has not the courage of facing death by killing. I would a thousand times prefer violence than the emasculation of a whole race. I prefer to use arms in defence of honour rather than remain the vile witness of dishonour.

8

A Wider View

THE CHAMPIONS

Me muscle 'n bone is all I own
I'm tops in de sportin' game
I like me own mission where I am king
All the blacks there know me name
Sure, I've come into some sort of money
An' I've got me own share of fame
Blacks ALL should work just like I do
Not be 'black power' lairs screamin' 'shame!'
Yellin' about black babies starvin'
It AIN'T no business of theirs!
I've built meself a good mansion
Don't tolerate 'loud mouthed lairs'
I've fought me way to the top, man
Me best friends are white — so I think
Black power-layabout drunkards
Raise up a needless great stink!
Sure, me home mission's just like a junkheap
Old shacks that a dog would sniff at
Black babies in filth there are dyin' —
But I used me bone an' me muscle
To get up here where I have got at!!

Very few blacks read, regularly and consistently, even about their own movement. One reason is that not a few are illiterate. It is this group whom Bobbi Sykes tried to reach and alert about the Embassy when she did her trip through the Northern Territory last year [1972]. Others, particularly the reserve- and slum-dwelling blacks of the south, can read because schooling was enforced. But many have never become adept enough at it to enjoy it and the content of an average newspaper is of no interest anyway, because none of it has any apparent bearing on their lives. For many blacks, life is extremely restricted. Most of the external stimulation that in a literate society is provided by books and newspapers is provided in the case of an Aboriginal by the people around him. Relationships, emotionalism, action and re-action, brooding about 'how to take' others' actions and comments — these fill out the day. 'The games people play' were never played so intensely and constantly as by Aborigines. That is why relationships, family and people — not the cold uncomprehending white man but real people — are so important to blacks. Only television has managed to crack this situation a little bit although, as with suburbia, the ABC is avoided like the plague in favour of the westerns and quiz games of commercial TV. Nevertheless, despite TV the average reserve black has the mental horizons of a Tennessee hillbilly. It could hardly be expected to be any different, although the youngsters are starting to wake up of late.

It is interesting, therefore, to see what an overseas trip does for an Aboriginal person, who may previously not have travelled any further than from Cowra to Walgett, or Townsville to Sydney. Travel broadens, they say. And of course, it can be a two way process. Last year Paul Coe travelled to Canada and America, expenses paid, at the invitation of an association of North American anthropologists covering both countries who were holding a symposium on the political struggles of native peoples.

> I was invited to present a paper. On the platform with me were people from Mozambique, FRELIMO as well as other

south-east African liberation movements. There were also American Indians. I explained to them that the Aboriginal movement should be classified as a liberation movement rather than a civil rights movement or a land rights movement and that in fact we had been colonised just as forcefully and arrogantly as anyone else in Africa or in the States. The only difference between us and the African people is that they happen to be in the majority. Therefore it is regarded as a liberation movement. We are in the minority. Therefore it is regarded as a civil rights movement. This is a point that is not clearly understood by most people and it should be emphasised. The reason why Papua New Guinea is becoming an independent nation is that they retained their culture and identity, and more importantly, they are still the majority. It is difficult for the white man to continue to rationalise his control when blacks are in the majority — as it is difficult for South Africa and Rhodesia to do so. It seems to me that the same principle could apply to Aborigines — who had their numbers decimated to a quarter or even less — if they weren't in the minority. Actually, the Aborigines' movement too, is a liberation movement. I think I made this point pretty successfully.

That was in Toronto. From there, I was invited to New York with the Black Panthers, with the African Information Service and representatives of FRELIMO. They took me around to the various programmes they had set up. I got an agreement that they would try to help us in as many ways as they could. They would try to invite more of our people over to spend time with them in the States and would try to send their people to spend time with us too. Both the Indian people and the Afro-Americans, the Panthers, stated that they would like to see an international solidarity movement developing between all suppressed peoples. In this movement, they said, the Aboriginal people would have a great part to play.

Both here and in Toronto, people agreed that the only solution to the problems of colonised peoples is an international solidarity movement to destroy capitalism, particularly American capitalism in the form of imperialism. It must also stop the advance of Soviet imperialism because they believe that it isn't much different from the American. Just a different name — both based on arrogance and greed. The solution is international revolutionary movements.

Bobbi Sykes, too, went overseas:

I've always been of the opinion that, because blacks are a minority in this country and because the media and the government is completely white-controlled, information about what blacks in this country are suffering is completely suppressed. When the opportunity presented itself to find out if this were so, and to attempt to correct it, I seized it. Primarily, I was asked to attend a symposium, as a journalist, in England. However I let it be known that I would stay longer if public meetings with blacks could be set up. I don't think that too many people in this country know that there are two million blacks in England. I don't think that too many people know just how many of them have applied to get into Australia and been refused. We still get almost only white migrants ...

In London, I talked about the existence of blacks in Australia — which most people didn't know about. I talked about the size of Australia. Most people thought it was about the size of Tasmania! I explained the geographic difficulties, how whites came to Australia, what they've been doing ever since they arrived, etc. I talked about the existence of black slavery in Australia, the bringing of kanakas [Pacific Islanders] to work the sugar cane fields, which no one had heard a word about. And the existence of reserves in Australia, the permit system, dual legislation and so on. Over there, there's great organised groups concentrating on abolishing just those things — in South Africa. I told them, 'you don't need to change your machinery. The same things exist in Australia.' They were all quite stunned. It was no surprise to find that the Londoners knew nothing. Lots of Australians attended the meetings, and they didn't know anything either. People would get up and say 'I lived in Sydney for forty years and I never saw any blacks. Are there any blacks in Sydney?' And I would say 'Yes, 20,000.' They would sit down looking stunned ... Everywhere I went, people were flocking to hear — the response was tremendous.

Bobbi's point about the repression of black points of view in the major Australian newspapers is one that I can support from my own experience. Before last year's Moratorium for Black Rights march on National Aborigines' Day, both *The Australian* and *The Sydney Morning Herald* refused to use a document I had prepared giving white people an outline of the *issues* that had led up to the march. *The Herald*'s chief-of-staff had been keen to get the material originally, as he was preparing a feature article on the Moratorium. Apparently he was dissuaded at the last minute. Similarly, I have found that TV stations edit and twist things out of context to give false, viewer-comforting news. Only pointless sensationalism and material that throws a humiliating and ridiculous light on Aborigines is given full coverage. The only group of newspeople that I have found to be an exception to this general trend are a tiny, radical group who somehow manage to survive in the ABC. As Kaye Bellear pointed out:

I think the reason people don't want to discuss things like black infant mortality is because, as whites, they have to do too much self-examining. I don't believe in it to the point where you have to beat yourself on the breast and say 'I'm guilty, I'm guilty, I'm guilty!' But let's look at the perpetuation of the system — because it hasn't really improved. Just because people aren't going out all over the country shooting blacks like they used to do — actually I'm sure they're still doing it in parts of the country, but they're not doing it in Sydney any more — that's no reason

> to suppose that things are much better than they were 100 years ago. Because I don't believe people are any better — people are just as bad as they ever were. And there seem to be very few whites who are prepared to sit down and really examine why it's like this and look at the history of it and talk about things like white supremacy and oppression. Wouldn't it be great if Australia was the first country to formulate some sort of educational programme for kids at school — where racism was talked about — where you started to stamp it out!

Before he did his university degree, Charles Perkins spent some time in England. Said he:

> The English people, on the race thing, were very good. Much better than Australians. They weren't so pig ignorant and hypocritical about it. I found it very good — probably the first time I felt comfortable. I have a gratitude to England for that. It was pleasant for me to be away from Australia and the race thing. But I noticed that the living conditions, in general terms, for the white people of the depressed communities in England — particularly in Yorkshire — are pretty tough. But, unlike our blacks, they've got their culture and identity and that is the difference. And so comparisons can be drawn.

Commented Bob Bellear:

> The thing is that blacks in Australia, the so-called militants, can't equate the problems in this country, the problems of class struggle, the problems of racism in this country with problems in any other part of the world. So they can't equate their problems with the problems of the North Vietnamese. And while people are being murdered, anywhere in the world, you must be concerned! The problem, of course, is getting blacks just to know about each other, in such a vast country as this.

After the Embassy had been ripped down, Chicka Dixon was approached and asked would he like to take a delegation of blacks to China. It was agreed and they timed it to come off just before the federal election.

> I was hoping the Libs would stop us from going. I knew it was illegal for us to leave this country in a delegation. Grassby spoke of this not long ago. He was going to get this law altered. Anyway, it was illegal. Had the Libs stopped us, it would've made a good pre-election stink, because we had already been invited by the Chinese people. The government didn't move, but Qantas did. They wouldn't accept the tickets. Yet they'd lost $2.5 million that year! So we went by New Zealand Airways. The excuse Qantas gave was that we didn't have any return tickets. But the PR man from Air N.Z. got in touch with someone over there who guaranteed the return tickets. So that fixed that.
>
> I'll be honest with you, I was a very frightened blackfellow going across that border. I've never seen so many guns. At this end of the border you've got British troops, armed. About 150 yards on, you can see them at the other end when you're walking through this tunnel — the Chinese. They're doubly armed. I got halfway through the tunnel and I said, 'Oh, jeez, a blackfeller'll never get home, here!' We'd never been in such a situation before.
>
> The Chinese were amazed at nine black people, from different states and none of us belonged to a political party! ... In Peking, a BBC correspondent got hold of us. We marched in Peking's Red Square, dressed in Mao suits and demanded land rights. That was beamed by satellite over to England, Canada and Australia. We put the Chinese right into the picture about what was going on. Infant mortality, the works. Wage conditions, you name it. We had blacks from different states with us. So when it came to wage conditions, we had the Territorian right with us. He just said how much he was earning a week compared to a white man. So it was a simple matter. The

bloke from Western Australia spoke about wages there and about the black population in jails as compared to whites. And we certainly learnt something about China, too. How they look after their old. How there are no babies starving like there are in Alice Springs. No old people going at garbage tins for a feed, like I saw in Australia. And the Chinese concept of communes and sharing. The old tribal fellow said 'Them fellars are like us, before the white man came.' So this was an eye-opener for me. We'd never been out of this stinking racist situation before. In China we were treated, for the first time, as human beings.

In 1970, Bob Maza, Patsy Kruger, Bruce McGuiness, Jack Davis and Sol Bellear travelled to Atlanta in the USA. Says Bob Maza of that trip:

> I met people like Jesse Jackson, Ben Johnson from the Panthers, Whitney Young, Ralph Abernathy. In Atlanta they gave me the opportunity to speak to 80,000 people. It was tough going for a while but then I warmed up and was doing alright. Then, during question time, they almost knocked me for a six when someone asked, 'What did they call Australia before the white man came?' I was completely rattled and all I could say was 'home'. Which brought a pretty good rapport. America is certainly a country I wouldn't like to live in. The tension there was just too much. It was getting me down. All of us had been so used to being able to talk to anyone we liked. But here we found that you just couldn't talk to white people, just because they are white. We found this pretty hard to cop. It's worse than being in a jail. Australian racism isn't like that.
>
> The black situation in the USA made me realise that if our black movement here in Australia is going to be left in the hands of whatever ego-trippers there are around, who are going continually to just use the situation, then we are going to head the same way that the black Americans

> did. As long as blacks with ultra-black ideas say 'OK, no whites, whites out, out, out, we do nothing with whites', then these people are certainly going to ensure that we are going to isolate ourselves. Isolation is going to put paid to any movement we might think we've got. It's good that black people should have a black-thinking appraisal of their situation, but they shouldn't get to the extent where they think they're the only problem on this earth. As long as they can see and think on a much wider scope.

As Lester Bostock pointed out not long ago, 'It's a bit hard for most blacks to get very interested in being involved in an Aboriginal movement. They're too busy just surviving.' Nevertheless black horizons are beginning to open out. In breadth of experience there is a vast chasm between a Paul Coe or a Bobbi Sykes and a Pincher Numiari or an Alice Briggs of Chapter 1. But Paul and Bobbi are the blacks of the future as education and a growing sense of black identity do their inevitable work.

9

Black Theatre

> Any political and social regime which destroys the self-determination of a people also destroys the creative power of that people. When this has happened the culture of that people has been destroyed. And it is simply not true that the colonisers bring to the colonised a new culture to replace the old one, a culture not being something given to a people, but, on the contrary and by definition, something that they make themselves.
>
> *Aime Cesare, speaking at the Conference of Negro-African Writers and Artists at Paris in September, 1956*

Black theatre as a cross-cultural development that is black controlled and black-directed, began in New South Wales in 1972 with the setting up of the National Black Theatre and its various workshops (dance, artists, writers, technical etc.) in Redfern. Its first presentation to the public was *Basically Black*, performed at Sydney's Nimrod Theatre in October '72. More polemics, admittedly, than theatre, it drew a mixed reaction from critics ranging from 'embarrassing' and 'basically bad' to 'a brave first effort' and 'an overdue, encouraging development'. After a season at The Nimrod, *Basically Black* went on tour, planning to show at settlements in Queensland and New South Wales. Director-actor Bob Maza told me the story:

To get the tour financed took a lot of bullshitting around as we had meeting after meeting with the men from the Council for the Arts. They knew about our tour some two months ahead and I told them, 'Now hurry some money through because we've got this Innisfail Arts Festival to attend and there's a possibility that we can take this tour straight down the coast and hit all the missions.' We needed enough money to cover against losses so that we could play at very low admission prices. The Council's bureaucracy was juggling us around right up to a week before we took off for Innisfail. So I borrowed the money from the other workshops in National Black Theatre — overall about $2000 — which was to get us to Queensland.

I made my great mistake by taking too many people on tour. There were thirteen, which almost ensured that there would be a loss. After our showing at Yarrabah, it looked like it could prove to be worthwhile at the missions, even at 20–50c a head. We wouldn't make any money, but we'd exist. Conditions were hard, though. There we were, thirteen people thrown together in a bus, camping on riverbanks at night and having to make do because funds were low. Really only six of the people were of the *Basically Black* cast. Three were needed for the extra work. Another one came along by invitation of a member of the cast. Another person I took along because she was having difficulties at home here in Sydney and I asked the group if it was alright if I took her along. She wouldn't get wages, but she'd get her dinner and help wherever she could. It would get her away from this particular situation she was in, which was pretty harsh for her.

The trouble really started before we even left on tour. I knew that the $2000 wasn't going to get us very far, in view of the expenses already, but I went on the understanding that money would be rushed through — which an officer of the Council for the Arts had promised. That would let me return the workshops' money and leave enough to tide us over for a month or so. Well, that money never eventuated. I feel that that particular officer reneged on the deal and ensured, as I say, by ploy or by accident, that the black tour would fail. The books are being audited still and there has been a lot of hassle about where the whole $2000 went. Consider that this is the same government that gives $40,000 for a bunch of footballers to go over to New Zealand to play, or $80,000 for four Aborigines to go with an ensemble to tour Europe. The whole thing backs up my scepticism about 'help'. Groups that do nice things, acceptable things, like play the didgeridoo in a concert for the Queen, or do a corroboree at an arts festival — for them there's plenty of money. But when you start making social comment, that's different. This is the same mob that are screaming about $2000 that a bunch of black people are taking up to give a show to other black people in another state!

The tour was a failure economically. But socially, I don't think so. Blacks who saw it up in Queensland loved it. It wasn't so good with the white people. A lot reacted against the show and its content and production. They weren't used to blacks talking like these young people on stage were talking — stuff on infant mortality, government harassment, government exploitation of blacks on missions. Most papers wrote it up as 'allegations'. Allegations! Stuff we knew was quite true! So Queensland whites are certainly not ready for this sort of gear. Which is all the more reason why it has to go back there. Even a would-be sympathetic little old theatre critic at Innisfail couldn't get over seeing blacks talking up like these blacks were doing both on- and off-stage.

But the white audiences' reactions were not to blame for the failure of the tour. The blame rests on bad organisation on my part, through lack of experience, lack of ability to coordinate people working together and an over-optimism which, I think, is a blackfeller's failing in this society. And, you know, doing stupid things like acting as a social welfare agency as well as a theatre. But I don't see any line separating these two areas anyway. I'm sure that if I had to do it again, I'd do the same. I'd still give a black person an opportunity to be a road-manager — give him a chance to prove his worth. Unfortunately in the case I'm talking about, the guy went up north and had a *week* to get something together. When you consider that people like Harry M. Miller send in a team of experts six months ahead to do their advertising ... yet the Council for the Arts virtually expected us to go up a week ahead, with amateurs and a shoe-string budget and succeed! I was aware of these pitfalls but I had one thing on my side that another type of theatre didn't have. This was that the young blacks were willing to starve and rough it, just to get that message across to black people on the reserves. But when the reality of the situation really hit them, things started to get pretty bad. The government should've had a little bit more concern, should've hurried that money through, should've made more information available about groups operating as we were. As it was, we did it all ourselves — cold. Which was a good experience. I don't regret it.

As I said, we didn't fail in the black areas. At Yarrabah mission they turned up holus-bolus to see us. It was the first time many of them had seen anything like it. Sure the whites were screaming about us up there, calling us radical Black Power theatre, shit-stirrers and whatever. In fact they wanted to have us stopped. I got this from one of the Labor people from a particular electorate around Cairns. But they couldn't hit us with anything because our language wasn't any worse than anything being produced in some of the bigger theatres around Brisbane. Had we continued, it would have been interesting to see how the whites would've reacted in places like Walgett, Moree, Taree and so on. The general reaction certainly proved that this theatre can be effective, if it doesn't gag itself and start doing the pretty little accepted things.

When we were showing at The Nimrod we had big houses, mainly I think, because there were a lot of curious white people who wanted to see what the blacks were saying, were doing. And it was a beautiful thing to see black people, who aren't normally theatre-goers turning up in the suit they were probably married in thirty years ago, to see theatre. And the kids who'd normally be going to the pub, coming backstage saying 'can we help?' 'can we work?' 'what can we do?' 'wa, wa, wa!' — you know? Black Theatre has tremendous potential. It can make blacks pull up and assess their situation, help them to think about where they are going, what they are lacking. Sure, a lot of traditional culture can't be put on the stage, especially the spiritual stuff. But a lot can and it will help blacks in the identity thing. In my view, Black Theatre should be aiming, for the time being, at social comment. Give on-stage blacks' views of the white society — the hard truth about its history, values. But we also have to attack apathy and laziness in our black society as well. Hopefully it will be a two-edged attack.

I believe that the Council for the Arts is going to encourage black writers. But they would immediately be put into a school that is geared to European theatre and they would be taught to write for white audiences. Then you get a conflict of presentation because a guy from the mission would write differently for his own people than he would for whites. So first of all Black Theatre has to figure out who it's going to play to. Then it should produce writers who are not going to write specifically for a white audience, but know how to put a play together. I don't know what it'll be like in the future, but I believe that so far, black writers haven't been encouraged very much because the people connected with the Commonwealth Literary Fund and whatever don't believe that Aboriginal people can contribute anything to the literary field. They don't realise that blacks talk on a different level on the mission. Your *Cherry Pickers* brought this out. A lot of whites would've heard this and said 'What are they talking about?' This shouldn't be jeopardised, it shouldn't be lost. This is the way we talk. Brendan Behan wrote the way the Irish talk … once the Council for the Arts realised that it's a real thing, it'd be accepted, this mission jargon. Sure *Basically Black* was more polemics than theatre, but with the necessary trials and experience, I believe a very professional theatre could develop from these young actors. They will quickly learn how to master theatre technique and use it to put over this reserve jargon — if they're given the chance.

10

Birth Control for Blacks

DON'T YOU TAKE THAT PILL
He tells me
DON'T YOU LISTEN TO THEM WHITES
THEY'RE ALL OUT TO KILL US, RACE-WISE
JUST TO SAVE 'EM SELVES SOME FIGHTS.
'MEMBER HOW THEY TRIED TO KILL US
POISONED FLOUR AND WITH THE GUN?
NOW THEY'RE OUT TO GIT OL' JACKY
WHILE HE'S AT HIS BIT O' FUN!
(How he bores me as he beds me —
Now if I could change their luck
I'd make every man among 'em
Have a baby — every fuck.
Soon we'd see 'em every morning
Like a boar-pig at its swill
Swallow troughloads while they're singin'
HALLELUJAH!!! for the pill.)

In Aboriginal eyes, the subject of birth control is an extremely touchy one. It is to be expected of a race of people who, not long ago, were officially on the skids i.e. 'dying out'. It is to be expected of a race of people who knew damned well that the white man was hoping that they wouldn't take too long about it. Of course the white man was proved to be wrong and now, despite a staggering infant mortality rate, the non-white population of Australia is reproducing at a rate much faster than the national average. Nevertheless black paranoia about suggestions from whites that they should embrace birth control continues to be strong, because of the suspicion that the white man's continuing interest is genocide rather than any concern for the quality of life of the black family. Also, it is a point of understandable satisfaction for most blacks to know that this lily-white, would-be homogenous society is saddled with an increasing number of blacks who cannot be kept out by means of White Australia policies or de facto White Australia policies.

Hordes of babies and small children are a feature of most Aboriginal reserves you visit and each new addition is generally welcomed by all. Yet new babies are often born into a situation that can't really cope with them. Because of such considerations, various states are working on providing Aborigines with family planning advice through their various health and welfare agencies. Predictably, blacks say that Queensland is less advanced than other states. Said Mick Miller last September:

> No attempt whatsoever has been made to get at these parents, especially mothers, about limiting the size of a family. Yet they know darn well that in many cases, the mother can't cope with another child. No help is given in planning a family. A woman might have six in six years. I know that some blacks talk about genocide and I see their point of view too. On the other hand, when there's a big family already and you know darn well that the mother can't cope with another one, or another two, it's just suicide for the mother! And the kids — the kids aren't benefiting at all! There's no way out but for contraception. I've stated this all along and I'll still say it. Because you see them — ten months in between — steps and stairs. And in a lot of cases, malnutrition and brain damage is very bad.

At Newcastle, Frank Roberts asked Aboriginal Affairs Minister Bryant whether it was true that the New South Wales government was, with federal encouragement, going to appoint an extra ten nursing sisters to teach Aboriginal women about contraception. In South Australia and the Territory, he said,

> health departments have already initiated such a programme — without consulting the Aboriginal people ... what they call a planned family. What we're concerned with is that it seems like deliberate genocide and will the Aborigines be consulted by the appropriate authorities?

Bryant replied that it would be a matter, he presumed, of individual decision.

> Strangely enough, when I was in a remote place called Jigalong in Western Australia, it was one of the questions the women raised. 'How do we control the number of babies we have?' There's a feeling around the whole world about it and we'll certainly give every assistance we can. Nobody's going to have these things forced on them.

As he pointed out elsewhere, family planning for blacks was just commonsense. No one can afford to have ten children these days and obviously the quality of life of Aboriginal Australians would be much improved if family planning was accepted. This was true enough, as Frank Roberts agreed privately later, but *he* had heard that forced programmes of birth control had been foisted onto the Pitjantjara people — in an area where infant deaths were already very high. It was this sort of thing that he questioned and he wondered whether it was true and if so, how far did the policy extend? In his view, one cannot argue with the social need for birth control, but, he felt, adequate consultation with blacks was the missing factor which made things suspect.

I wonder whether people such as Sir Macfarlane Burnet realise the reaction they cause in blacks' minds when they say things such as the following, reported in *The Australian* (22/3/73): 'Aboriginals must limit the size of their families if Australia is to avoid racial problems like those in the United States.' The black reaction? Buggar Australia's future problems; buggar *us* having to stop breeding to make life more comfortable for the gubbah; buggar *us* having to limit our population because whitey is a racist. Let the *gubbahs* stop breeding then everybody's problems, white and black, will be solved.

Bobbi Sykes touched on another aspect of this idea:

> As long as Australia still wants migrants and is willing to pay to get them, I'm not for black birth control. If they want more people, then let them encourage the original people of this country to breed up. Let them encourage it with more endowment, grants for big families and so forth.

Which mightn't be thinking that is quite in the Arthur Calwell tradition, but fairly puts the black reaction to migration and contraception.

Many Aboriginal women have an aversion to any form of contraception, including the 'pill'. As one said recently, 'I'd rather be fat every now and then than fat all the time.' Others, of course, are hampered by ignorance. They may be interested in having less children, but have no knowledge of birth control methods or how to get the information. Some time ago an Aboriginal woman told me about a black women's conference that she had attended in Sydney against the wishes of her husband, several years ago. She was pretty disgusted about the whole thing. She had been lectured at for several days about contraception, pre- and post-natal health care, a balanced diet for self and baby, care of the baby and so forth. She said she had tried to argue with one of the lecturers, Dr Clair Isbister, who, she thought, might know what she was talking about for white families, but was just talking nonsense from *her* point of view. Soon after the conference, with its exhortations still ringing in her ears, she had fallen pregnant again. And no, she hadn't applied any of the things she had learnt. She couldn't because she lives on an Aboriginal settlement way-a-way out in the west of New South Wales in a one-roomed tin shack with a dirt floor and a kero fridge that mostly isn't working. Balanced diet is impossible. You eat what's going when it is going which, in turn, depends on the availability of 'bush tucker' and a welfare cheque. That particular settlement is dominated by a remarkably strong matriarchal rule. The older women are boss and it is *they* who say how children are to be brought up and treated, regardless of whether their methods would be approved by a Dr Isbister. The older women are also totally opposed to contraception. The younger woman would like to avoid having more babies but mother-in-law says 'no'. And that, out there, is that. There's not a thing she can do. Her husband is completely mother-dominated. She cannot get to a doctor. She has no money. She is trapped. All she can do is keep on having babies.

Most of the better educated blacks do admit, at least to other blacks and in private, that family planning advice is needed in many parts of black Australia. Occasionally one of the younger articulate blacks does send up a scream about genocidal plots but of course when this happens, it is always a male — who doesn't have to do the bearing of the children. One can suggest, and responsible blacks do, that some of the excess energy expended by these young blacks would be better turned to providing some support for the various black babies they leave around the countryside for someone's grandmother to rear. Suspicions of genocide aside, the need for birth control is a very real thing. Blacks cannot expect to 'advance' materially while they have huge families. Not even whites, in a much more advantageous position in the economy, can support ten or twelve kids adequately. But logic is one thing and the emotional block against birth control is another — and it continues to be a very strong one. Soon after the appointment of Elizabeth Reid as Gough Whitlam's adviser on women's issues, a newspaper columnist contacted various women's organisations for their opinions as to what ideas they would like to see her submit to him on subjects of interest to women. Replied Pam Hunter for Murawina, a Sydney-based black women's group: 'Recognition of black women of Australia as being breeders of a race that intends to keep on breeding.' So there.

II

Four Points of the Black Compass

THE PRICE

Price of survival
Where are the songs of old
The customs crafts and old corroboree
Where gone the different ways that all unknown
Was flooded down the years of time by tears
Where is the difference
My people dance
Not to the droning pipe but jukebox clear
Price of survival.

Price of survival
Where is the lives of old
The laughter joy and old security
Where gone the tribal life that kept me well
Then left me to spiritual penury
Price of survival.

Price of survival
Where are the dreams of old

The hunter songmen and their sad ballet
Where gone the artist with the law all known
Who drew the dreams of life on rock and clay
Where is the difference
My people mourn
Not for the death of one but death of all
Price of survival.

The Kooris, or southern part-blacks, can be placed into four broad classifications. First, there is the 'mass' of fringe-, slum- and reserve-dwellers; unassimilated, distinct from the rest of the community and easily distinguished by the psychological condition of its members. Second, there is the small group of 'assimilated' blacks who lead normal private lives in much the same way as other Australians and who have similar values and a similar outlook. Third, there is the politically and socially conscious and active 'radical' or 'militant' group and fourth, the politically and socially conscious and active 'conservative' group. Of course such categories are at best crude tools by which to classify anything as complex as human beings. For example, someone may be 'radical' where the noise is and 'conservative' where his pockets are; or you may scratch a Black Powerist and find at best a fool or at worst, a coward. Nevertheless, these four categories will do for our purposes.

Category one, the 'problem blacks' are, as a general rule, pretty limited in their experience and outlook. They are shrewd enough in their judgements about anything that impinges on their daily lives but find their interests almost exclusively within their own experience, gossip and the doings of their immediate neighbours. It is people like this who will switch off a television programme devoted to Aboriginal affairs because it can't hold their interest. (I've seen them do it.) With the exception of, perhaps, one or two in each community (there is always someone) they know very little about the Aboriginal movement, its aims or achievements. 'Black Power' is something frightening because it might bring trouble. The white man as policeman, boss, rent-collector, welfare man and bully in a thousand forms casts the central shadow on their lives. Many are born, almost, with an inferiority complex. Insecurity of employment, of income, insecurity about not being able to pay the rent and the consequent threats of eviction, welfare action against their children, police victimisation, delinquency — all these things are common. Caught in a vicious circle of poverty, irresponsibility, despair and apathetic resignation, they prefer to stay on the reserves because the outside world looms too large, too threatening.

The second group, the 'assimilated' Aborigines are the group you never hear anything about. They are usually fair in complexion — Aborigines are not likely to be readily assimilated if they are too dark — and while they may or may not identify as Aborigines, they do not make a feature of it. In this category are the small shopkeepers, fishermen, miners, farmers and ordinary working class Australians who happen to have had one or more black forebears.

Category three — the politically and socially conscious and active 'radical' or 'militant' group — generally called the Black Power sector, the shadow of things to come. Of them Professor Wootten of the Aboriginal Legal Service said,

> There is now a new breed of Aboriginal — the angry, articulate young men and women, proud of their Aboriginality, deeply concerned for their people all over Australia, quick to resent patronage or condescension and to suspect racial prejudice, determined to demand justice now, and unwilling to be put off once more by waffle and promises or to fritter away their energies on fruitless delegations where they obtain a perfunctory hearing and no results ... I see in them the great hope of removing the stain of Aboriginal degradation from Australian society. They alone have the enthusiasm, the courage and the eloquence to overcome the apathy and selfishness of white Australians and to unite their own people all over Australia in a great forward movement.

The 'radicals' have mostly lived on the reserves themselves, are pretty closely in touch with the conditions and feelings of the reserve people (even though they mightn't always report these feelings quite accurately) and are often only younger, more aware, more vocal, more active and less crushed versions of typical reserve people. They yearn, in varying degrees for *more*, not less black identification and have shown an interest in recapturing facets of their decaying Aboriginal culture. When Pat Eatock returned from last year's FCAATSI conference at Alice Springs with a tribal slogan — *Ningla A-na*! ... hungry for land! — for the Moratorium for Black Rights, she was responding to this need for a return to the traditional roots and language.

Category four — the politically and socially conscious and active 'conservative' group — is the one that, in terms of influence, is the strongest. It has its entrenched representatives in the major Aboriginal advancement organisations (most of which advance only their employees), the public service and lately, thanks to the Liberal Party, in the Senate. Many who fit into this group are fairly 'acceptable' in white society and as a result, show a characteristic ambivalence — they do not know, quite, whether they want to be white men or black men. Many conservatives are openly contemptuous of Aboriginal culture. They have usually imbibed slabs of Christian fundamentalist doctrine in some form or other and tend to consider the Aboriginal 'clever man' tradition as nasty, superstitious and primitive. Knowing nothing of the practical wisdom and acute psychological insight of the clever men or the grand good sense of much of the tribal custom and belief, the prevailing feeling of this group regarding its racial background is one of shame and embarrassment. Because there is no ultimate emotional pride in and loyalty to the black tradition, there is no great sympathy for the black predicament either. And certainly no sympathy for other blacks' desire to return to traditional things for another look, for guidelines to the future. So, Neville Bonner told a no doubt enthralled Senate Committee not long ago that 'there is a lot of Aboriginal culture that should go by the board'. Given twentieth century realities, this might, in fact, be true. But whites have denigrated the Aboriginal culture enough already without a black adding his bit. Therefore, Nev, that is *not* how an Aboriginal patriot speaks.

On the face of it, a conservative black is a bit of a contradiction in terms. What have blacks got to conserve, for God's sake? But that's it, in a nutshell. Conservative blacks are conserving jobs, positions and security like hell, because for each one there is, right at the other end of the line, the memory of that mission. So you take a mild position in black affairs because that is sure to please the white boss. You talk a lot about black peccadillos. It's the way to get on. You demonstrate your 'reliability' and your 'responsibility' even if, once you've got a niche, you mightn't ever again do a tap of real work. What it all boils down to is that you demonstrate to everybody that you are as good as a white man. It becomes an ego thing. It is understood only too well by all blacks how tough it is to get a reasonable education and a decent standard of living. Therefore anyone who manages these things tends to consider himself pretty special — especially if he can forget how he had to arselick whites on his way up. Now he has proved that *he* is not an ignorant black, no, *he* is different and he proves it daily. Any blackfellow can do the same, if he will only stop being so contrary and work his way up 'like I had to'.

Says Paul Coe, law student, and identified with the 'militant' group:

> The colonisers have everywhere used a buffer class to suppress black people. For example the Indians in Africa have been used as a buffer class. In the States, middle class negroes are being used as a buffer class to keep their own people down. It's a grave danger and I can see the possibility of it developing here. In fact it has. FCAATSI and the Foundation for Aboriginal Affairs are typical institutions where the white man is using blacks to suppress the Aboriginal people and stop their true opinion from coming through.

In this sense, Coe would typify Neville Bonner as a member of the 'buffer class', a 'Tom'. Far from being proud of Bonner as the first black member of parliament, many blacks have become alienated in the extreme by the statements that Bonner *will* keep making. Blacks suspect that he is a stooge being used by the Liberal Party to show Australia, tongue in cheek, its commitment to blacks. When Bonner makes statements like, 'I hope the new Labor policies do not try to sweep away all the discriminatory legislation for Aboriginals', or 'Aborigines get a better deal in Queensland than in any other state in the Commonwealth' or 'The Queensland government is doing everything in its power to help the Aboriginals' — blacks puke. And can you imagine how Aborigines in the audience must have felt when, in the course of an address on 'Aboriginal Land Rights' to the Sydney Law Society, Bonner (according to the draft of the speech which he later sent me) told a rapt audience that, 'What I am to say will shock your legalistic and wondrously logical minds'? (The whites who weren't laughing must have been thoroughly flattered.)

Blacks also suspect that he talks the way he does because it is the Queensland government that finances his black advancement empire, the One People of Australia League. Nevertheless, at times he *does* change course and speak well for his people; for example, when he said that until governments recognise Aborigines' rights of prior ownership, 'everything else is charity'. Or when the Embassy was pulled down during parliamentary recess and he stated that he was 'disgusted with the federal government's actions'. But he wouldn't, subsequently, move on the issue of undue police violence against the defending blacks. It is not surprising to me to hear that a black champion like Senator Keeffe has been known to make loud raspberries in Bonner's general direction. As Bonner himself has complained, neither Bryant in this government nor ministers in the previous government ever bothered to consult him — their very own resident expert on Aboriginal affairs! It must be a lonely, powerless feeling when, as Bonner has complained, Senators pointedly ignore him in committee rooms.

At times, Bonner says damn silly things like 'Aborigines don't need special representatives in parliament', or 'It's not true that Aborigines are oppressed'. The latter statement reminds me of part of Bobbi Sykes' 1972 pre-election prayer which asked

God to 'turn Messrs Hunt and Howson into black women and send them into the creek-bed at Alice Springs'. I wouldn't be surprised if she thinks Bonner would profit from a spell there, himself. As a woman, of course.

Predictably, Bonner feels that it is going to take generations to advance blacks to any significant degree. (I certainly bet he wouldn't agree with me that on black land, properly funded and imaginatively handled, a major change could be wrought within one generation.) Hence, like so many conservatives, he accepts the white-imposed order of things and exhorts his fellow blacks to join the system and work up. Or, as he put it on ABC television's *Monday Conference* on May 7, 1973, speaking to some of the Redfern blacks: 'Because I've worked through the white man's system, I've got into a position to do something for Aborigines.' It is true enough, if he actually *does* help blacks (and cuts out propagandizing for Bjelke-Petersen). But what he forgets is that many of the young militants *reject* the idea of crawling through the white system because *they reject the system itself.* And how do you tell some of the reserve blacks — who have learnt years ago that no matter how they try, *they* never get any further anyway — that *someone* did manage so how about they try again, a little harder? That is the trouble with many of the conservatives; *their* immediate problem has been solved, so the problems of other people don't seem so pressing either.

Perhaps the best comment of the night was made on *Monday Conference* by a young Queensland Aboriginal, Ross Watson. The 'confrontation' between Bonner and his audience had been pretty tame. Even though most of the blacks in the hall were hostile, not very interesting questions had brought not very interesting replies until, towards the end, Ross Watson got mad at the pussy-footing drift of things. He got to his feet in an attempt to bring the meeting round to the emotional guts of the Aboriginal situation. But his feelings had got the better of him to the extent where he could not develop his ideas into a coherent address. It didn't matter. Because the confrontation was live, because Ross was spot on emotionally, the effect was magnificent as he said:

> I mean we're not getting at the issues, you know. The issues, the real issues, you know; I mean you look at any park; well I just come down from Queensland and it's the same down here, you know, see where the blacks are. Look in any of your prisons, see what percentage of blacks you've got in your prisons, you know. This is what we're talking about, you know. Your black kids that are dying. Don't sit here making apologies, you know, and passing issues off. The black people are oppressed; they've never been part of this white system, and the way things are going they never will be ... There's a race of people, Senator, we're fighting for our lives; we're fighting for the right to get up and live how we want to live, you know.

The effect was beautiful. The raw emotion conveyed much, much more than any polished speech could have done. Every black in that hall knew what Ross meant, alright, and so did Bonner. When he couldn't go on any more, Ross Watson turned and walked out of the hall. It was a pity that the rest of the audience didn't have the wit to follow him out.

12

The Leaders

He came from the North
A leader.
He came from the West
A man.
One sold his own for a song and dance
The other, a big brass band.

Aboriginal leadership is an amorphous thing. At the local level it still tends to be exercised by the older women, so continuing an old local tradition of Aboriginal life. I remember the influence exerted by my own Aboriginal grandmother at Condobolin some twenty years ago. What Ellen Naden-Murray said was well noted by all the Condobolin blacks and she used the weapon of Aboriginal 'shame' to devastating effect against whoever she felt needed it. Besides the authority of women like her, there was no discipline in the black community at all, except the discipline exerted by an external white force, the police. Within her community, Ellen's influence extended into everyday matters such as standards of daily conduct, the behaviour to be expected even of a drunk, the treatment and bringing up of children, the moral conduct of teenagers and so on. It even extended to adjudicating domestic disputes between husbands and wives. When necessary, she was in the habit of reinforcing her authority with a powerful left hook. She was six feet tall and weighed around 196 lbs. (The famous 'Mum Shirl' of the Aboriginal Medical Service is not unique. Shirley Smith comes from a long line of strong-minded Aboriginal women.)

This type of inner community control still exists in most Aboriginal communities at varying levels of success or lack of success. Without it and without the 'shame' factor in Aboriginal relationships there would be near anarchy because there is just about no other control left, in the south, anyway. Yet the value of this matriarchal control is limited. The older women are themselves products of a long decayed society and therefore show all the limitations of that society. Often illiterate and conditioned by all the negative prejudices of their experience, they cannot provide community leadership of a type which will introduce positive changes for their people. Occasionally you might see an academic this, or an educationist that doing his damnedest to buck them up and prove different because he's got a pet theory and perhaps twenty years' standing as a Great Educationist swinging on the outcome, but on the whole he'll end up admitting that he can't get them to organise themselves to the point of providing any sort of leadership anyway. That's what you get for 'being and doing' for blacks. Real leadership must come from younger Aborigines who are more sophisticated in their understanding of how to manipulate the mechanisms of the white society.

What sort of leadership is there in the black community? Probably the best known Aboriginal organisation is the Federal Council for the Advancement of Aborigines and Torres Strait Islanders. It has the best contacts amongst unions and politicians and the best access to funds. It is also considered passe, at least in New South Wales. For a number of years now, virtually its only contribution has been the organisation of a series of costly conferences which produced much rhetoric and impressive resolutions but very little follow-up. Of course conferences help to promote black solidarity, but in black progress, the action has come from other quarters.

In Frank Roberts' view:

> Most Aboriginal organisations are out of touch, out of feeling. They do not conform to the principles of Aboriginal opinion and they just pick themselves at random. The basis of leadership should be an elected leadership by the Aboriginal people themselves. There must be Aboriginal involvement and there must be Aboriginal participation at every level. FCAATSI does not fill this role because it is not even a state organisation so how can it be a federal Organisation? It does not reflect the Aborigines' feelings at grassroots level. For one, it has never approached me and I am sure that there are tens of thousands like me who have never been given a chance by FCAATSI to express their view. The need exists for an Aboriginal national body expressing Aboriginal needs and viewpoints. FCAATSI could never become such a body because an Aboriginal organisation must be composed of Aborigines. Any organisation in Australia works like that — the RSL represents ex-servicemen — each represents their own. FCAATSI is multi-racial. I've got nothing against multi-racial organisations but when it comes to the question of Aboriginal rights, I think multi-racial organisations should be prepared to take second place. If FCAATSI is allowed to influence the new government's Aboriginal policy too much, we must condemn it. I think then that the Aboriginal people must become ruthless and destroy such an organisation, which only projects its own image, and not that of the Aboriginal people as a whole.

In New South Wales, at least, FCAATSI is not only out of touch with grassroots opinion but is a totally unfamiliar organisation amongst the people it supposedly represents. Its orientation appears to be strictly a gubbah one, and upper middle class gubbah at that. Like so many Aboriginal organisations it has long since become the private preserve of individuals who are more characterised by their cynicism than anything else. In Aboriginal affairs there are many such organisations. They play a role, certainly, but they are essentially non-representative, although some are better than others.

Then there are the 'leaders' in government employ. It may not be altogether fair, but in black eyes nevertheless, anyone who takes any type of government or semi-government job automatically becomes suspect. The money–fear–security nexus that seems to be the backbone of these jobs sooner or later prevents black employees from acting in the black interest, no matter how much 'on side' they might feel. They can, perhaps, go so far, but definitely no further. There are examples of blacks in comfortable jobs for years by virtue of their ability never to upset the white bosses. These are called 'reasonable blacks' by some and 'Uncle Toms' by others. Cynicism is a strong feature of their personalities, not to mention a kind of obsequious venom. Blacks know them from long experience. They know that black patriotism and a fat wallet cannot and do not go together. As Pearl Gibbs, that old die-hard Aboriginal patriot put it:

> It suits the government to pick out certain blacks and put them into important positions. They've got one thing in common. They're all as weak as piss. They get big money for selling their own people down the river.

This has been a recurrent complaint amongst blacks. Their most promising leaders have been lost to them because governments have tended to employ and so buy off any black talent. It was a recognised way of nipping any potential trouble in the bud. If the Labor government could overcome the widespread distrust of black public servants by allowing them to speak out and fight for their own people, it would be one hell of an achievement.

Aborigines have not taken kindly to those in their midst who have assumed to be 'leaders'. A strong reason is a uniquely Aboriginal individualism which does not accept the right of anyone to speak for them without long and exhausting prior consultation. Decisions tend to be arrived at by group consensus and are then adhered to — no matter how idiotic or impractical they may be. (It will be interesting to see how young Aboriginal 'leaders' who say they want to return to the umbrella of group consensus and consultation with their elders swallow *this* pill!)

Another reason why blacks have not taken kindly to would-be 'leaders' is because they feel that they are being 'used up' by those leaders. For example, the conservative leaders tend to show an opportunistic respectability that becomes a fine point of bitterness/mirth for their Aboriginal brethren. Extremely conservative themselves, the black majority nevertheless resents those blacks whose conservatism expresses itself in white terms. A group of blacks were in attendance at the Eucharistic Congress earlier this year, in Melbourne. One of these was Bob Bellear:

> I thought Frank Roberts was on side! The night before the joint conference, he called a meeting with selected people in groups and the workshops. I was one of them. We discussed how if there was a panel elected from us and not *by* us then we'd boycott the meeting. Now Frank Roberts wasn't even a delegate. And yet the day the joint conference started there was a panel sitting out in front of everybody and who was on the panel? Pastor Frank Roberts! And when it was time, when we questioned the panel about being selected by the hierarchy and not by us, he denied everything. He just wouldn't stand up and be counted. He just sat there and was given this sheet of paper to read about his state. It wasn't compiled either by him or by us! It was compiled by the bloody organisers of the conference! And he was prepared to stand up and read the stuff that was compiled by them. We had no say. So we just got up and walked out.

And why wouldn't it be like that? Frank and other conservatives like him do their best up to a point. But they have a family to keep and they know how easy it is to get out of favour with the white power structure.

In Frank Roberts' own words:

> Aboriginal leadership must become autonomous. They must establish a base, a moral ascendancy. I think that the Aboriginal has got to respect and encourage Aboriginal

> leadership. It must, firstly, be an Aboriginal leadership that knows the inner feelings of the Aboriginal people. Secondly it must come from amongst the people. And thirdly, it must be independent of governments.

It's fine. It's true — especially the last sentences. But independence takes money and that is the catch in all Aboriginal affairs.

Another reason why leaders are generally either laughed down or pulled down is because not one of them to date has, in the Aboriginal estimation, lived up to an adequate standard of personal integrity. And this call for integrity is one thing that has not been popular amongst the young leaders ... or the older ones, come to that. So, one would-be leader is rejected because he is over-fond of skirt and tries to use his prestige to get it. Others are rejected for bellowing about the infant mortality rate when everybody knows damn well that they themselves have walked out on young children. Another one can't make it because everyone knows that the old fox has, for years, been supplementing his income from Aboriginal funds whenever opportunity allows (at the same time yelling, full voice, 'Feed my black brothers!'). Aboriginal patriotism, ersatz, can be a lucrative thing if you've got the stomach for it. Another would-be leader keeps his habit going by selling drugs to other blacks and bludging off black working girls. Another sells his arse for drugs and money — a back entry into society?

One and all, black 'leaders' face the problem — independence and a lean belly or a job that confers an income while at the same time robbing the black of his autonomy to speak and write as he sees fit. Some blacks hover in a no-man's land in-between — making pseudo-radical noises while making sure that enough effusive praise is being heaped upon whatever Canberra black is pushing their barrow for them. That is why some blacks prefer to shy away from public service jobs or Canberra patronage — they prefer their freedom. Gary Williams is one. He won't even start to have anything to do with it, or hasn't to date, anyway. My feeling is that it is OK to take a government job, provided you are prepared to stick to your integrity once you've got it — not, once that's known, that there is any real danger of being given a position anyway.

When you consider that a full participation in Aboriginal affairs can easily involve you, in Sydney, in having to attend anything from one to four meetings per night, every night, plus having to deal with correspondence and one hundred and one derivative jobs, it is easy to see why to do it at all properly, you have to do it full-time. Which is fine, while your money lasts, and tough after that. A minority try to earn sustenance part-time or full-time to fund their activities in the Aboriginal movement; at best a bit of a losing battle. Others, again, manage to get themselves on scholarships and live that way. Those who can't or won't do any of these things get out of the movement, if not sooner, then later. Whatever way you look at it there are sound reasons why Aboriginal 'leadership' is so amorphous, so unstable. And the reason behind all other reasons is lack of money. Lack of the money that will confer black independence. (Although, of course, the Faith'll always be kept, baby.)

How then is whatever leadership that is at times shown, achieved? Some Aborigines get funds for travel, conferences etc. by crawling to the unions. And I say 'crawl' advisedly, because that's generally what it takes. Others appeal directly to the public and get a measure of support that way, as the Embassy did. Others tie themselves up with government grants. Others live on the dole and move around the hard way. Others, as I said, bludge. Economics being the first of two reasons why there is no stable leadership at either national or state level, spokesmen, rather than leaders emerge and disappear. There is always informal leadership of a sort and whoever is spokesman for the time being voices things that are consistent with the broad sweep of Aboriginal opinion because the basic gripe never changes. Money, too, is part of the reason why there is no nationally united Aboriginal body that is independent of white control. There are no Aboriginal businessmen able to put a few thousand dollars into any all-black representative organisation. There are no sources of reliable and recurring finance, other than government grants — always given with the inevitable strings and controls. I can't see any government, regardless of political colour, resisting *that* temptation!

Commenting on the humiliating fact that there are lots of things in Aboriginal affairs that blacks themselves do not have accurate, up-to-date information on, Paul Coe said recently:

> We've got to do some research into these things ourselves, before we can really comment on them. That means sending some of our own people into these areas and finding out what the hell is going on. We are not in a position to do this yet. But we will get to the stage where we start to accumulate a certain amount of capital so that we do not have to depend on white professionals, white experts or even the federal or state governments for charity. Then we will be able to put our own people into the field and find out what the hell is going on.

It seems to me that an (uncensored!) weekly news-sheet, distributed free to all blacks all around the country is the outstanding obvious need. Instead, we have *Identity*, a government-funded magazine which doesn't even *begin* to do the job it should be doing (and which, I bet, will soon once again be under a white editor). I hope Coe is right about being able to accumulate some capital. God knows, I've seen him at enough meetings planning something and being frustrated at every turn *because there is no money.* Until such time as blacks have this capital, to fund their own autonomous projects, they're going to have to swallow the gubbahs' whims, vetoes and directives. In other words, until that ship comes in (no madam, we're *not* cargo cultists as well) the dominant theme in Aboriginal affairs will continue to be one of powerlessness.

The other major reason why there is no stable leadership in Aboriginal affairs is the human, all too human one. Aboriginal life is an ocean of suffering, maladjustment, ill-health, dreadful conditions, stunted, wasted lives, dying babies and frustration. On top of this sits a ramshackle superstructure, Aboriginal affairs, which can be described as a fishbowl full of conflicting egos and ambitions all swimming around, flat out, bumping into one another as they vie to be top 'Saviour of the Race' in much the same way as you every now and then see a white man trying his hardest to be 'Great White Father'.

The bitchy world of Koori politics is quite as deadly as anything seen in white politics. 'Leaders' who have attained some degree of preeminence will go to extraordinary lengths to ensure that nothing threatens them and can be seen virtually elbowing each other in the rush for TV coverage. If there is an offer for several blacks to go overseas to address some people interested in Aboriginal affairs the 'leaders' either go alone so there is no rival for the publicity, or else they take care to pick only those blacks who won't threaten *their* glory. The name of the game is kicks, publicity and jaunts. (Travelling is usually regarded as a 'jaunt' and is called that.) It is not unusual to see what little Aboriginal money there is funding jet-flights and motel expenses for a totally unconstructive 'jaunt' by some notable. Similarly conferences. There is always one being held somewhere, funded with union money. Most of them are useless because they are not held on a big enough scale and are therefore in no way representative. There is little follow up from them — often resolutions are not even presented to the authorities. The attitude that it is only gubbahs' money and therefore it doesn't matter is all very well, but there is only so much of that money and *it could be going to a much better purpose*. The catch of course is that the gubbahs' money is at the disposal of whoever has raised it. *He* calls the tune. Say a conference has been arranged at the other end of the continent. There is so much at hand for fares. Accordingly, the New South Wales delegation will be composed of Number One and say half a dozen deadheads whose only qualifications need be that they are black, like to go on the occasional jaunt, and haven't the intellectual capacity to bring up any real ideas that threaten to put Number One in the shade.

In typical Koori fashion, 'leaders' size each other up, probing for weaknesses. Most Aboriginal organisations are the preserve of one man or woman who either runs them single-handed or else puts in a 'safe' staff. Obviously the 'safest' blacks are those who are direct family or friends from back home because these are a known quantity. That is why so many Aboriginal organisations become, say, Cummeragunga preserves or Cowra preserves or whatever, that freeze out blacks from other areas. It is family loyalty, too, that ensures that no matter how lazy, untalented or heartless someone may be, you will see that person being put up, time after time, for new positions in Aboriginal affairs. In the absence of family and friends, other Kooris, who have proved that they will not think independently and have proved their willingness to kow-tow and flatter Number One are chosen.

Within this magic circle of safety the chosen ones continue to jockey for position. Remember when certain Sydney blacks tried to howl down the formation of the Legal Service because it didn't suit *their* ambitions? Remember when a certain notable tried to create an empire in Redfern with loyal support from big brother? Remember the blacks who spoke against the Redfern Community Housing Project because they weren't on the committee? Why are things so deadly? Because for many, Aboriginal affairs is the only avenue they are ever likely to get for participation and self-expression. There is no alternative. The prize, of course, is to land a job in Aboriginal affairs, because then your life's interest becomes your income as well. Most blacks are poor and unskilled. Only in Aboriginal affairs are these two attributes forgiven you. Working in the black set-up is a lot more congenial than working in the outside world and it generally pays better too. Ask Len Watson whether the livin' is easy. Ask Charlie Perkins what it was like in the periods when football or black affairs weren't funding him.

It is the need to put 'safe' people into key positions that explains why Aborigines do not make more use of whatever meagre scraps of talent they do have. It explains why generally you won't find your best or most experienced black actors in theatre groups; why you won't find your best writers being utilised; why you won't find your most humane blacks in welfare jobs; and why you won't find your best intelligences on consultative committees (although, thank God, there are *some*). Personal ambition, too, has so far successfully resisted the formation of a successful, nationally united Aboriginal body. There is an obvious and crying need for it, but each time the call goes out, it founders because at that particular time it doesn't happen to suit the current fine-angling of a Charlie Perkins or a Gordon Briscoe or a Jack Davis or a Frank Roberts, or a Chicka Dixon or a Faith Bandler and so on. No wonder Kath Walker, after struggling for years, just wanted to get away and write poetry somewhere!

Because so much of the leadership is one of cunning rather than commitment and everybody knows it, there is a great deal of disillusionment, cynicism and despair current. It can be seen even in the 'aware' blacks who are themselves playing the game most keenly. Some argue that it is unrealistic to expect black people, or black politicians, to be any less corruptible than white politicians. Others argue that at least whites in this country have solved most of their own most urgent social problems — it's black babies that are dying, not white ones, so at least until *this* situation has been fixed, *why not* expect more from blacks? Why not call for a higher standard of personal integrity and discipline?

Some blame that handy old scapegoat, the white man, for all perceivable black failings. Commenting on the back-biting and personal rivalry so prominent everywhere, Gerry Bostock said:

> This is a bloody big problem. It's one of human nature. One of the Anglo-Saxon human nature that's been educated into blacks by the white society. What they've got to do is get a whole new indoctrination to overcome this thinking that has been forced upon them by Europeans and then unite all blacks together so they're not all going in their own separate directions for the same thing.

Paul Coe, who dreams of a separate state for blacks, where, somehow, with the white man no longer in control, a new innocence, a far better state of affairs shall prevail, was asked why it was that in Haiti, a self-ruling black state, things were in such an appalling social mess. Said Paul,

> Well, I think mainly because, uh, well ... black men, like white men are ... many are the same. Many have learnt

> the greed and arrogance of power and want to accumulate more power in order to suppress their own people.

It is time that a bit of the truth about this sort of thing is faced by blacks. Certainly most of us believe that the tribal way of life was a superior way of life, devoid of the competitive, sharking ruthlessness required in white society. We believe that the old Laws were just and wise and good and provided an umbrella for the growth of the human spirit. Certainly most of us believe that it was not until the white man came that greed, lust, arrogance and meanness came to the Eden that was Australia. But time has not stood still and we are not as we were once. It is what Aborigines have become, at all levels, that we have to start being honest about and this honesty is going to hurt.

Although Paul Coe did say 'uh, well' etc., when faced with the fact that human nature is pretty much the same everywhere, we have to remember that he also said,

> Certain black people have not learnt to respect history. I think that the time where economic or political power is concentrated in one man's hands should've passed by now because that system doesn't work.

Of course it *does* work, but only for the ruling individual — as so much of Aboriginal affairs factually demonstrates.

And yet, and yet ... there *has* been growth in all this. Growth for black people. I am willing to stake my last bean that there has been more growth for black people in the last two or three years than in almost two hundred years of previous white rule. The steps forward to date have been halting, stumbling. But they have been taken. Blacks must continue to struggle to get that white man off their backs. And to achieve that *will* require a nationally united body that can turn those tentative steps into a stride.

13

Love's Labor's Lost – the reality of the reserves

PHASE OF GLORY

The pipe of my people drones a sombre song of sadness
And it echoes o'er the valleys and this wide
Sunburnt land
And it cries to me in sorrow
With the tears of the forgotten
Who wander
Landless nomads 'cross their father's rugged land
And the song that they are dreeing
Seems to throb to life a being
In my mind's eye an image in a sad corroboree
In this land there is no portion
Not a camping place to rest on
For the gubbahs greed has swallowed all
In his voracious need.
Took the country of my people
Stole the mountains and the valleys
Stole the grass and stole the streams that flow
So coolly to the sea
Stole the blackman's land and manhood

Stole the very spirit from him
Left him nothing,
Rubbish nothing
Only left him tears to dree
Now we're crying and we're dying
The oppressed, the chained, sob-sighing
While the gubs are calmly lying
'Land of hope and land of glory
Southern landfall of the free'.

Of course, there were the Australian racists who turned up and said, 'Oh, but blacks drink too much', and 'Why are all the blacks in Alice Springs drunk', and 'But Aborigines let their children die. They don't take them to the hospital!' Which points are always extremely hard to answer ...

Bobbi Sykes, discussing her 1972 lecture tour in London

The one unmentionable that black spokesmen all keep a determined silence about is the undeniable degree of black culpability in their own day to day situation. I am referring here to blacks who have been colonised for several generations ... those tribal folk who have only recently come in from desert areas are totally victims and can bear no share of the blame. But the 'old hand' of several generations must bear some of the responsibility for his own condition or else human adaptation and character has no meaning. Many blacks, even at the most sophisticated level, would, as the saying goes, break your heart. And if a quarter-caste woman spends all her income on taxis and grog while her kids starve and get sick, then I believe that it is a matter of private selfishness and corruption rather than the fault of any larger racial issue — although the latter has undoubtedly contributed to the situation. The subject is an extremely complex and subtle one, difficult to attempt to analyse or write about because the causes of it are deep rooted in white/black history and psychological interaction. It is easier, I think, for a white man to write about the black situation for he either takes a 'they're bums' attitude or, alternatively, a *mea culpa* line.

Personally holding a brief for neither race when it comes to human weakness, corruption or cunning, I am in a less favourable position to write clearly on the subject. Jail tends to make one quite a student of human nature and yes, the disgust is pretty evenly distributed between white and black, even though the sympathy tends very much more to the black side. It is possible to see the scum everywhere, white and black, what each is trying to swing and the games that are being played. That is why, sometimes, I have to laugh a little at some of the American Black Power rhetoric. It is all true enough, as far as it goes, but of course it never tells the whole story — the complementary tale of black trickery and back-sliding. Perhaps it is just as well. Give the white man an inch and he, master of hypocritical double-thinking that he is, will take a mile. So let nothing that I say here about black culpability be used by any white man to excuse his own grasping, mean-minded inhumanity.

Of course the Aboriginal image has been so debased, humiliated and foully stereotyped that Aboriginal spokesmen are often seen to be reluctant to admit to any human failings save that of powerlessness in black people (except in private). To do so is seen as disloyalty which only serves to reinforce the stereotype of Jacky, or else sheets too close to home some particular failing — always a threat. As a result, there is an exaggerated refusal ever to admit to any of the aspects of the stereotype that are true. Accordingly, the further investigation of causation is never attempted; the idea is blocked. Imagine, then, how far the black community is, psychologically, from a realisation of the need not only to face and cease condoning their own gutlessness, but from a realisation of the need for community self-discipline and total community organisation. It is so much easier and less painful to project this energy out — into hatred for the white man. He becomes the universal scapegoat for all black failings.

It is, of course, important here to stress strongly the distinction between detribalised and tribal Aborigines. The latter continue to have a strong check on individual behaviour even when they have already started to a degree on the detribalisation skids. So, one of the Gurindji Campaigners tells a story of how three Gurindji decided that they would leave the tribe at Wattie Creek and go and work for Vestey's. The Elders threatened to 'sing' them if they did so. One returned to Wattie Creek. Of the other two, one had died and the other was sick at the time I was told this story. This type of control is occasionally used in far less tribally cohesive communities and is very real. On the other hand, many detribalised blacks on southern reserves have almost totally lost their Law. White police provide the only control on their behaviour. Many blacks of this sort function pretty well entirely on undisciplined emotion, behaving exactly like chickens that have been let go with their heads cut off.

The long-term effect of detribalisation and the concomitant loss of self-determination by blacks has been appalling. Generations of dreadful social conditions and dependence on 'handouts' has sapped the initiative and the substance of blacks. The resultant apathy is understandable and is continually reinforced. Remember the story of how Aborigines camped in the river bed at Alice Springs requested an ablution block? (Change the locale and the details a bit and it is a frequent tale.) Apparently they accepted the fact that they had to live in knock-up humpies which they had to crawl into on all fours. They accepted, it seems, the constant fact of social disadvantage and ridicule. Perhaps they even accepted the fact that black girls as young as ten years of age need to become prostitutes to get a crust — or the fact that some of their men could be seen selling the use of their women to white men for a flagon of wine. For a little while, so goes the story, the people figured that at least they didn't want to pong quite so much. For a while, the ablution block probably became a symbol in their minds for all the rest of it. But Alice Springs is a developing tourist centre. It's embarrassing to see those blacks camped as they are in the river bed. Why encourage them by providing an ablution block? When blacks already at a psychological bedrock meet this type of resistance, they give up quickly. They have found over and over again that it is crazy even to try. Then, when a white man, good-doing, arrives to test out a theory, he gets no response. Why? Because they don't believe him, they've heard it all before when it also didn't work, and the thing is couched in terms of *his* values and seems pretty irrelevant anyway.

Is it any wonder that for many blacks grog has become the central fact of life? It provides enjoyment, release and finally, oblivion. And so the thing rolls on. That is why last year, London BBC television producer Bob Saunders, on a visit to the Alice, remarked:

> You Australians should throw out the Aboriginal Welfare Department and send in the Red Cross. The Aborigines in Alice Springs have the status of animals. What everyone seems to forget is that these people are Australians ... There is absolutely no excuse for people being forced to live like this ... They are a people stripped of all dignity. It beats me how people can peddle the Aboriginal folk lore in the shops on the one hand and kick them in the guts on the other.

Besides the 'kick in the guts' that every black around Australia is well familiar with, there is the factor of loss of culture, loss of a positive identity. Can a sacred site, revered from time immemorial, really be that special, asks a tribal youngster of himself, when a white man comes to no harm after bulldozing his way through it? Can a tribal elder have very much prestige when whites call him 'Jacky' and laugh at his drunken reelings? And what real wise man will pass on the precious teachings to confused, cheeky, headstrong youngsters? A woman who has had considerable experience as a teacher in the Northern Territory told me of her impressions. The Darwin blacks, she said, are so screwed up that all she could do for them was to let them talk it out, while she listened. At Hooker Creek the prevailing fact of life is aimlessness, purposelessness, frustration. Only at Wattie Creek was there a different atmosphere. Sure conditions are tough, she said, but the people showed the comparative contentment that a sense of purpose brings.

The loss of a sense of purpose is the outstanding characteristic of most of the southern blacks also. For as far back as they can remember, things have been stacked against them. For generations now, Aboriginal men have received no wages or inadequate wages or have been unemployed. Few have been in a position to be providers. Dependency has eroded the position of men in the family. Indeed, many Aboriginal women would, economically, be better off without a husband. That is why it is no tragedy when an unmarried mother has a child. She is no worse off than she would have been had she been married. It is possible to go around the reserves on pension day and see young, healthy, chronically unemployed men standing over mothers and old pensioners for grog money. Curiously, from an outsider's point of view, the dependency of the men is encouraged by Aboriginal women. In European society women will discriminate against loafers, winos and down-'n-outs and soon relegate them to the park bench. Yet their black equivalents are highly likely to be protégés of some Aboriginal woman who can be seen pampering and making excuses for them. Perhaps they do feel sorry for them, as one black woman told me was so in her case. Or perhaps it is because these men need the help of a woman desperately and the women respond because they, in turn, need to be needed — even if the ultimate price they have to pay for pandering to the man is no money for food and the kids in welfare homes.

The reader has to understand here that I am talking about a cross-section of reserve men. There are, of course, many Aboriginal men about whom none of the above could be said; indeed, it would be a slander. Many of them are definitely *not* bludgers, no-hopers. But many, in turn, are. A sub-cultural ethic, almost dictates that such a man does nothing but drink, fuck and fight. A life devoted to these things is somehow admirable and is considered so even by many of the better educated young blacks. Police coercion is the only discipline. Without it, the reserves would, in many places, be total anarchy. There are places in New South Wales where all hell breaks out on Friday night. The entire reserve area is a shambles of drunkenness, fighting and bedlam. Children move from house to house and from bed to bed in an effort to keep clear of the drunks. In one town in New South Wales some years ago, a well-intentioned city do-gooder was sympathising with an Aboriginal father who was being railroaded out of his own home by the local welfare officer. The do-gooder went to great lengths to spell out to the man what his civil rights in the matter were. But, as the exasperated welfare man pointed out later, the point at issue was not the father's civil rights. The point was the continued *survival* of the man's children; he became temporarily insane when in drink and had already seriously injured his children on several occasions. These are the types of things that are the nitty-gritty that black spokesmen will not touch on. Like the story of the black who punched his heavily pregnant wife, already the mother of eleven, into an induced abortion and then went to the pub to share the joke with the boys. Until blacks create a type of community control that will obviate the need for police control, the discipline that white police exert will continue to be needed. The fact that the *need* for police coercion is very often parallel to the *fact* of unfair police victimisation of the black people is, of course, another story.

Because unfair discrimination by white people against blacks is so universal, it has also become a tool which blacks use to dodge responsibility. The cry of 'discrimination' is a fine defence against having to grow. So, an Aboriginal youngster might be facing an examination for which his teachers have been coaching him for months. He can't face it and does not attend the exam. To the blacks he explains that he has, once again, become a victim of discrimination. This will be absolutely believed by all his family and neighbours. It is human trickery, not racism that is at work, but who is to point this out? As far as the blacks are concerned, it is just another confirmation of what they already know — that they can't make it. I know of at least three cases of Aboriginal men who suffer permanent physical crippling as a result of injuries received when they were blind drunk. Each one either blames the cops or the white man generally for his condition. None of them accept that it was his own irresponsible stupidity that ruined his body. One of them reckons it is the white man's fault because he brought wine into the country! So growth is avoided and this psychological buck-passing occurs amongst all levels of blacks.

Many blacks live only for now. The feat of marshalling a fortnightly pension over a two week period is too much for them and the second week is often a desperate time. When food is bought, it is highly likely to be potato chips, soft drinks, cakes, biscuits and lollies, Weet-Bix, bread, sugar and jam. If meat is bought it is usually tinned, or devon. If anything is cooked, it will usually be fried. Anything that is wanted is bought on the spot, irrespective of price, poor value or next week's needs. This type of improvidence is most felt, in due course, by the children. That is why Dr Coombs, in an address to the Australasian College of Physicians on June 5, 1969 was able to say:

> If an Aboriginal baby is born today, it has a much better than average chance of suffering malnutrition to a degree likely to handicap its physical and mental potential and its resistance to disease. In childhood, the person would suffer a wide range of diseases. In adolescence he is likely to be ignorant and lacking in sound hygienic habits, without vocational training, unemployed, maladjusted, and hostile to society. In adulthood he is likely to be lethargic, irresponsible and poverty-stricken, unable to break out of the iron cycle of poverty, ignorance, malnutrition, ill-health, social isolation and antagonism. And so the wheel will turn.

I don't think that many white people have much of an idea of the pitiful mental level at which many detribalised blacks function. Generally isolated at school (which they leave as soon as possible), made to feel inferior by society at large, ostracised for real or imagined lack of hygiene (blackness *is* equated with filth) and given no avenues of self-expression (bar, occasionally, in sport), their world is bounded by the first reality in their lives — the reserve. They are 'different', they are 'Kooris' — people with only a vague and confused memory of long lost tribal standards. Usually only negative legendary remnants of tribal lore have survived — a dreaded being who inhabits a certain swamp here, spirits of the night there, a giant killer dog somewhere else. The fear is strong and the tales haunt the people as they have always haunted backward country people of all races. Then there are the memories of how white men massacred their people here, raped there, tortured somewhere else. The spirits of the blacks who died are still about; they are not at rest for there is no rest in horror.

Fear too, is part of the cement that binds the people together. It is the basis of reserve horror stories about what 'they did to us'. The other night there was a knock on my door. It was a young Aboriginal chap from a nearby reserve who had set out from a town only fifteen miles away at 11 a.m. that morning to hitchhike home. Nobody had given him a lift. As a result he had found himself in my area, still four miles from home, at nightfall. By the time he knocked on my door, his whole body exuded fear. 'I'm frightened', and would I drive him the rest of the way home? Does it explain, in part, why these people need the security of their own, why they can't leave a reserve to live elsewhere, except in company? Why the reserve, however hellish it is, is still a familiar comfort? Anyone who remembers being scared of the dark as a kid will understand alright.

As I said, life on many reserves is bedlam. One must admire those who nevertheless manage to keep to decent standards in the midst of it. On the whole, children of any age and either sex come and go as they please. There are no regular mealtimes and often no meals as such. Everyone grabs whatever food is around when it is around. Often houses are not lived in — they are 'camped' in. On many reserves, women spend a good part of their time gambling. At Bourke Reserve, where there are no houses at all, only appalling shanties, it is not unusual for bingo to start at 10 a.m. and continue until nightfall. The women sit in the open, in the dust, ignoring the squeals of hungry or quarrelling babies. Drinking, gambling, these are the means of social stimulation for those who have not become 'Christians'. And they, in a way, have given in to the pressure of white mores. As Kaye Bellear said of her goomies:

> They have got far more black identity than any of the militants, the radicals. My theory, and it's just my own theory, is that the reason why a lot of the gooms drink is because they won't cop white society. They just refuse to accept it. So they stay outside it. And their way of expressing this resistance is by drinking metho. Because they just *won't* be assimilated.

This rejection of the whole white system is one of the underlying reasons — besides budgetary improvidence — that explains why rent collection is such a difficult thing on most reserves. At an emotional level blacks wonder why the hell they should have to pay rent for what are often sub-standard homes to those who stole their country from them. Australia is a black man's country, mate. You mightn't realise it, but *they* do. Is it any wonder that they resist your rules, your dishonest little demands, your rules that are one thing for those with money and quite another thing for those without it? Is it any wonder that they refuse to be 'responsible'? That they drink themselves into oblivion rather than face their own impotence and humiliation any longer?

As blacks will tell you wherever you go: 'We once had a Law. It was a good Law. It was a clean Law. If you did something wrong, you got it, no matter who you were. Everybody knew this. You didn't get away with anything in those days. Not like the white man's dirty law which can be bought for money ...'

I write this after returning from seeing a black woman who told me that last night a reserve girl, aged fifteen, was raped. She was returning home with a group of other girls after the pubs had closed. All had been drinking. A white man pulled up, on the hunt for some black velvet. When he couldn't get any of the girls to enter his car, he jumped out, grabbed one of them, took her up the road and raped and beat her. The other girls fled. Passers-by later found the girl by the side of the road. They took her to the hospital and the hospital authorities informed the police. The police took the girl to the police lockup and kept her there overnight. The girl has since been sent to a home and no action has been taken about the rape. As it is the third time recently that reserve girls have been raped in this area and the complaint received by the police with indifference, blacks are saying that it is stupid to appeal to the law in this country because you only get yourself into more trouble.

So the black man spits on the white man's laws. And his own Law is pretty well dead in the south. When I was a child, I remember how black law-breakers in the Condobolin area were still dealt with. Say someone had interfered with a child, or habitually beat his family. He would be warned, several times. If he did not stop whatever he was doing, he would, one night, be taken down to the river for a party by other blacks. He would happily get roaring drunk with his uncles and friends and then be quietly drowned in the river. It was, perhaps, crude but justice was done. It happened on several occasions in my memory.

But such discipline is rare now. Reserves are split into factions and the splits are deep and bitter. Families may have lived near each other for generations, but one lot is, say, Catholic and the other lot is Protestant. Groups may have different racial origins. Or one group may have been in the area three generations less than the other group and is never allowed to forget it. In most country areas there is a rift between the town blacks and the reserve blacks. The latter are jealous of the superior material status of the town lot and deride them for being 'flash'. The town blacks, in turn, resent the overt jealousy and strike poses of superiority and deride them for their 'laziness' etc. On reserves, whatever one group decides to do will almost certainly be automatically opposed by another group. After all, 'who do they think they are?' The black children cannot be controlled by anybody, except whites. Any attempt by a black to reprimand someone else's kids for misbehaviour or vandalism brings quick trouble from the offended parents. The kids know this and take full advantage. Adults have no status, no authority. Many of them are as childish in their thinking as the children and cannot arbitrate between them in a reasoned, adult way.

Life is a perpetual round of being 'done to' by the white man, and an equally constant series of tricks to avoid being done to. For example a black may have bought himself an old car which he hopes will keep him going for a while. He may have driven for twenty odd years but hasn't got a licence because he has reason to believe that it wouldn't be granted or else the difficulties of application, the procurement of 'L' plates and 'P' plates etc. are mysterious and insurmountable. But he gets by because he obeys the traffic rules as far as he knows them and he doesn't get caught until one night he is picked up for d.u.i. and being an unlicensed driver. This costs him, say, three months in the cooler — which worries him not at all because life there is no worse than he is used to and at least the meals are regular. As soon as he gets out of jail, he will do it all again, as long as he can get away with it. The whole elaborate exercise of 'punishing' him has achieved not one whit and life goes on as usual — dodging the white man and his rules.

One of the preoccupations of New South Wales state governments in their dealings with their black charges has been the desire to *force* them to be 'responsible'. So, administrations will go to incredible lengths to collect rents on reserve houses, not so much for the bit of money involved, but because blacks must be made responsible, in white terms. Blacks must pay regular rent, for this is an important step in the official 'assimilation' process. Black uselessness cannot be allowed to prevail. On the other hand, there has always been resistance to rent paying on Aboriginal reserves. At the black level of thinking, there is no justice in having to pay rent when they should be paying *us* for what they have done to us. At the level at which the administration functions, the refusal to pay rent once again shows black obstinacy. Accordingly the blacks must be coerced. Coercion in New South Wales, under Aboriginal Affairs Minister Waddy, has meant lots of threats to evict with an occasional eviction carried out to show 'em. On the black side, resistance has been constant, based on a mixture of resentment, fear, inertia and race hate. Underlying it all is the universal Aboriginal sense of the enormity of the complex of injustice that whites represent.

The unlikelihood of such conflicting assumptions ever bringing about the development of real human growth are obvious. Rent paying is an unjustified affront to the Aboriginal people. But if we assume, for a moment, that it *is* justified, then we can analyse how white/black interaction contributes to the continuing immaturity of many reserve blacks. I have in mind a case of an Aboriginal woman who is a prime example of irresponsibility and immaturity. Her kids are on a bond for being neglected but this has made no difference. They are still neglected. Mum *would* feed them if she had any money when they come crying to her, but usually she has already spent it on grog and taxis. The best she can do, therefore, is to send them to scrounge off neighbours and take their chance that way. Apart from her improvident drinking habits, this woman has a number of teenagers bludging off her. Between one thing and another, she is not able to feed the babies too regularly. How much less is she able to pay rent? Eviction notices have made life insecure and the insecurity has caused more visits to the pub.

In a more coherent, traditionally stabilised community, women like her would be made to toe the line by means of group censure. Assuming that rent paying were defensible, she would be *forced* to pay the rent. She would be forced to care for the children. The almost constant neglect of the children would not be tolerated. But reserve blacks are not a stable society. The woman concerned is able to get away with it because the older women share her weaknesses and have long embraced 'minding your own business' as the best way to react. (And let the devil take the kids.) So not only does the irresponsible get away with it, but other blacks actually help her, support her in her actions — because all are united in an unspoken resistance *against the demands of the white man*. Much as they might deplore her neglect of the kids, it is the *white man* who charges them with being neglected. It is the *white man* who says that you shouldn't drink. The *white man* wants his rent paid. So there is this unspoken sympathy mixed with their condemnation, for if it is her today, who'll it be tomorrow? There may be much verbal criticism of the woman, but nobody *acts* to censure her for shucking off her responsibilities onto others.

It is the total structure then, of white/black interaction, that has a lot to do with keeping blacks down. Another factor in it is the famous black inferiority complex. I notice in an article about Tony Mundine in *The Sunday Telegraph* (27/5/73), that Tony's grandfather at Baryulgil, Harry Mundine, was described by one of the uncles as a man of strong character, a 'real white man'. *The Australian* (29/5/73) carried a letter from an anti-racist reader objecting to the ABC playing the song 'Brumby' on its hospital session in the mornings. Brumby's 'skin was black but his heart was white' go the lyrics and the letter-writer objected to it being given air time on the grounds of taste and because of the disturbing inference that 'the attitudes and assumptions implicit in the song are tacitly accepted at all levels of Australian society'. Of course they pretty well are so accepted and by nobody so thoroughly as the majority of blacks. It is not uncommon to hear Aborigines in the south refer to themselves as 'the rubbish'. Such is the self-image that they are heir to. This, after generations of white control, white paternalism. Surely it must now at last be starting to come home to whites that their style of administration will *never* do away with 'the black problem' as the assimilation policy was meant to do?

Reserve blacks are on the increase and mightily perpetuating their kind — new generations of misfits no use to themselves, each other or to society. Even if there are jobs, many won't work because why work when your cousin who is on social services gets very little less than you can earn, for doing nothing? It is only when there is work for everybody, as a community thing, that blacks will not tolerate shirkers. Occasionally a big family might go after seasonal work. Together they might earn $300–$500 in one week. Gambling will soon have them broke again. Why save it? If they bring any money back to the reserve it will soon be gone, in handouts to relatives or to supplement the dole they have to be on the rest of the year because there is no employment in those parts. Besides, what would they put a few hundred dollars into? They have no land, no identity, no pride of race and consequently nothing to build for, save for, work for. So why not splurge it and have some fun while you can?

The New South Wales government believed that it could get rid of the Aboriginal problem as we know it by gradually phasing out reserves. The idea was to throw blacks into the general community on a sink or swim basis. With white neighbours on either side, it was felt, the blacks would shape up in white terms; become imitation white men because they would be away from the comforting company of their own. Up to a point this works. But in many cases it doesn't. Many blacks can't forget their roots; they still live with the legacy of victimisation. I do not know of any part-Aboriginal who is not in some way, however assimilated he may be, affected by what is behind him. The direction my own life has taken and the things that have happened to my family are in no small measure a result of the black blood in our veins and all the implications that this black blood had for us. That is why land rights as symbol is so important. Land rights as symbol and substance of the fact that some amends to that black blood are due. After agitation against New South Wales state government attempts to sell off black land, the government framed legislation to give New South Wales blacks around 6000 acres to be put under the ownership and control of an all-Aboriginal Lands Trust. It was a start, but time revealed that there were all sorts of catches and exceptions to the thing that made the mean little crumb of 6000 acres even meaner. And it appears that a federal government won't be able to get around it without at the same time raising all sorts of sticky states' rights versus federal rights questions and involving itself in legal tangles. Imagine them tackling this for the sake of blacks!

Out of Australia's sad and inhumane past a people are slowly limping home to a state of justice. The crippled, the alcoholic, the retarded, the victims are slowly shedding the oppressive cocoons of 'protection', 'assistance', 'welfare' and 'assimilation'. (Memo Mr Bryant: let's *actually* plough the 'assimilation policy' once and for all?) Slowly the people are beginning to insist that the white man keep totally out of decisions that affect them. If there is to be a regeneration of blacks, it must come through self-determination, however hesitant the first steps. The only thing that years of white administration have proved to us is that it doesn't work, it can't work. Mr Giese and Mr Killoran could keep it up for centuries and still it wouldn't work, even if for no other reason than the 'do unto others' one.

Whether development of the black community can be any better achieved by blacks is of course another question. White critics cite the 'fact' that blacks won't take orders from blacks where they will from whites; that black managers in the old days never did as good a job as whites; that a black man needs a white boss. And so forth. I personally believe that everything depends on the nature and quality of the control that blacks have to exert over blacks. Blacks are always probing and testing each other for weaknesses and using these weaknesses for their own short-term advantage. That is why so many blacks in controlling positions are so ineffective. Also, everywhere you look, you see blacks attempting to put their own family into key jobs in Aboriginal affairs; or if not the family, then a tame dog who will toe a safe line. Before meaningful black self-rule can come, I believe that Aborigines who now hold controlling positions have to do a lot of re-thinking on this subject. When you see the results of this type of patronage in the field, it makes you wonder what on earth the blacks have done to deserve their leaders.

What about an eventual re-building on the reserves? Mr Bryant talks about appointing 100 liaison officers. Hang liaison! What about giving these officers the training and the facilities to enable them to approach the people with more than words? The words they've all heard before. Any black who approaches his own people with ideas of helping them quickly discovers his own impotence. He quickly discovers that he can 'stir' but he can't really help them. Take my own experience. Asked by blacks for help, I did what I could in terms of letter-writing and advice. Then the people begin probing for weakness. They decide that you want to make a big man out of yourself. They are quite willing to give you the ego-rubbing they think you want, provided that when they descend upon you for petrol money, bail money, a handout here and a sling there, you don't say 'no'. It's too bad if you can't, in fact, afford it. If, on top of that, you start pointing out the discomfiting ways that they *could* be helping themselves, your popularity wanes quickly. For when it comes to the crunch, it is handouts that they want when they say 'help'.

I started an art class and discontinued it when I was not able to keep on paying for the materials needed. My various attempts to get decent art equipment received no response. This is not in small part because I am hopeless at asking for things. Apparently the thing is to move in stages, not asking for too much at a time and genuflecting at appropriate intervals. Temperamentally I can't manage it. (A lot of blacks are pretty good at it — half their luck.)

As soon as the black 'helper' runs out of dough, his feet of clay show clearly and scorn is heaped upon him accordingly. Not that a piddling art class even begins to get to the root of anything anyway. And the people are right to sneer for it is *action* that they see so little of. Only a black working at it full-time, who has the kind of support from government that allows him to effect *real changes*, material changes on a reserve, will be able to command the cooperation that will allow him to begin real community development. And then it can't become an exercise in how to be popular, either. A black community organiser will be in a unique position to begin to motivate these people. He will be in a unique position to point out the spongers. He will then be in a position to call a spade a spade without the people being able to use the 'discrimination' defence. On one reserve I can think of, several groups are engaged in a struggle for control of federal funds that have been allocated to them. Each faction is as impractical and impotent as the other. Only a properly trained community developer could break the impasse and move towards some sort of group consensus. And in the long run it is only group agreement and the constructive operation of the 'shame' factor against laziness and neglect that is going to make the crippled ones shape up to normal adult responsibilities. For ultimately, it *is* the unmentionable things, the things that black 'spokesmen' like to avoid, that have to be brought out into the open for examination by blacks, for blacks.

14

The Anatomy of Black/ White Interaction — a closer dissection

This chapter turns out to be the last one that I write and that in two stages. The first part of it was written some three months after I had written most of Chapter 6, entitled 'An Act of Faith', and the second some four weeks later, at the end of July 1973. It deals with the same subject as Chapter 6, the Redfern Aboriginal Housing Project, and describes developments in the organisational structure and aims of the project.

It is always difficult to attempt to comment on current happenings and this chapter has been bedevilled by rapid changes at the housing project while the book has been in its pre-printing stages. But as I pointed out in the Introduction, fine detail does change rapidly in Aboriginal affairs; it is the gut things, the underlying principles that I have tried to analyse as clearly as I am capable of doing. It is these principles which can be seen to be operating in Aboriginal advancement empires right around the country. It is these principles that will endanger the spirit of future housing projects (and other similar grassroots developments) unless they are clearly understood and recognised for what they are by Aborigines everywhere.

I have decided to leave the first part of this chapter unchanged as I wrote it in late June because that was how facts stood at that point in time. Reminding the reader again that details are one thing and the underlying principles are another, here then is what I wrote in June.

*

Recent developments in the organisational structure and aims of the Redfern Aboriginal Housing Project provide an excellent case history which shows clearly how deadening and corrupting any sort of white interference, even well-meant interference, in black projects is. It also serves to point out clearly first, how important it is that blacks get their values straight and second, why it is so necessary for a white man's act of faith to be *total* if it is to have any meaning.

It is important to remember that the 'Aboriginal problem' is *not* the presentable black who ingratiates himself with the white boss. (Well of course he *is* a problem, but of a different sort.) The Aboriginal problem is the underprivileged, the homeless, the destitute blacks. Yet wherever you look, you see not the black needy being helped but the 'decent' blacks who are willing to take the white man's orders; to bow to his value judgements as they use the aid or development programmes as a personal or family gravy train while proving to the white man that they, at least, are as good as the white man.

The original concept of the Aboriginal Housing Project was of a place where the city's destitute, homeless blacks could come for shelter. It was not to be a handout centre. Each and every person, including the goomies, were to pay some rent (out of the social services or pensions that Bob Bellear was trying to get for them) so that there could be a gradual return to pride in self, a return to self-value as a human being. Everybody was to share in some responsibility around the place so that a feeling of belonging would be generated. Late in March, after hearing so much about this wonderful new hope being held out to blacks in Redfern, I travelled to Sydney to interview some of the people then camping in the old houses in Caroline St. There I met the goomies. (Several of them turned out to be relatives of mine — uncles and aunts.) All were bubbling over with the knowledge that for the first time in their lives they belonged somewhere and, guided by Bob Bellear, they could help build something of their own. Sure, they were drinking but it was controlled drinking according to their needs as alcoholics. Ruined, pitiful human victims they were, yet within each of them you could see the hesitant, glad response to the first bit of meaningful aid offered them. Enquiries around the place revealed that external control by blacks was needed at times, even though the gooms were trying to be cooperative. Several of them tend to be violent when in drink because their entire lives have consisted of nothing but violence and horror and a similar response is now conditioned in them. Nevertheless they *were* capable of being handled, provided the control imposed upon them was firm, kind, understanding and non-provoking.

The original concept of the housing project was also that it should become a beautiful experiment in black self-government that could be run *without white control* and so become a symbol of pride for blacks everywhere. This concept has been thoroughly white-anted before it even got off the ground. In Chapter 6 I wrote that the project could either become a sterile 'better blacks' residential' or else it could become 'a true social experiment, a commune incorporating both traditional Aboriginal life styles and European ideas into a synthesis that has meaning for both races. It can become a place that lifts the horizons of all blacks who go there.' Well, thanks to the usual white-anting from various quarters, it looks pretty well as if the 'better blacks' have won once again.

The scene for this was set by the enormous amount of publicity generated by the development of the housing project. A mass of editorials, feature articles and letters to editors ensured that the project was well and truly surrounded by a miasma of white opinion even before it had properly got going. Next, the opposition of Redfern locals and various elements both in the South Sydney Municipal Council and the Labor Party hierarchy was publicised. The whole thing then created an enormous wall of white opinion which said that blacks were about to form a black ghetto, a brawling, boozing brothel which they themselves would not be able to control. How the blacks involved in the project got sucked in by these attitudes and how they became corrupted, both by them and by their own lack of standards, their own lack of firm values, is the theme of this chapter.

As soon as the first home had been renovated, Dick Blair and his family moved in. Now the project was intended for homeless blacks and Dick Blair was not homeless. But he *was* a committee member and he *did* keep order. So, OK. Dick, by this time, had gone into a complete tailspin on the 'we'll show the whites' thing and had had considerable press and TV coverage denying that blacks would lose control. After the press had done its best to stir the racial trough in April, Bob Bellear suggested that to cool it, they should put a complete ban on all further publicity. The very next day Dick went on television once again to assure a startled nation that yes, HE WOULD CONTROL these blacks, never fear. And so it went on and on and on. More newspaper interviews, more TV, more Dick Blair in the limelight.

Remember what I said before — that no black who retains his integrity, his loyalty to the black people, can last long in Aboriginal affairs? Well, Bob Bellear is the latest victim. During the spate of publicity in March/April, Bob and Kaye had been engaged in a series of running tiffs over details with a Mr Dick Hall who happened to be the minister's personal representative in Sydney. They felt that he was trying to steer the project away from its original ideals so as to conform more to white ideas of what it should be. It soon became apparent that Bob Bellear, from an administrative point of view, was not sufficiently amenable to control from above. Dick Blair on the other hand was making all the right noises — a much, much more reasonable black. It was around this time that Bob Bellear was replaced by a black vote as president of the Aboriginal Housing Committee by Dick Blair.

When the second house was ready, Kaye tried to get it for a woman, an old age pensioner who is currently paying most of her pension for an appalling little flat. The woman had some family with her and was desperate for space. Nevertheless, Dick

Blair's brother moved in instead, even though he was earning something like $100 per week as a builders' labourer on the housing project site.

Next, the Aboriginal Housing Committee decided that all people who got behind in their rent would be evicted, hence ensuring that only able bodied working men could live in the development. Any ideas that Bob had been cherishing to get the gooms onto social services or pensions so that they could afford to pay some rent thereby went down the drain, because his scheme required a bit more tolerance than that. Down the drain too, went Bob's dreams of helping the maimed and crippled who need it most. I think that the heart pretty well went out of Bob and his wife at that point.

Which left the field clear for the 'decent' people to move in. People who *already* have homes, who *already* have jobs. The professional Aborigines. Blacks who want to show the gubbah that they are as good as he is. One of Dick Blair's favourite TV/newspaper phrases during the spate of housing project publicity was 'it's the first chance we've had in 200 years'. Chance for whom, Dick? For you? For your family? For your friends? For blacks who are comparatively well-off already but who want to climb just that little bit higher — on the backs of their brothers? Remember how 'decent' blacks (with the usual white aid) buggared the Foundation for Aboriginal Affairs? Is *this* project to be yet another swindle on the people? Another family empire that doesn't do its real job?

What was the nature of the control that blacks were exercising during the formative period of the housing project? How was Dick Blair fulfilling his promise to white Australia? The Aboriginal Housing Committee formed an Action Committee made up of Dick Blair and five other blacks. This was to be the police force. After the Director of Aboriginal Affairs, Barry Dexter, had refused to buy them special uniforms to dress up in, they resorted to red arm bands to show everybody just who they were. Then they set out to 'control' their own.

In jail you live with the constant sight of screws bashing defenceless prisoners who cannot and are not allowed to defend themselves. You see, acutely, the terrible weakness of weak men in strong positions. 'Power corrupts' is an old truism. How much more then, do you think it can corrupt men who have been powerless all their lives? Now I'm not for a minute denying the need for discipline and control in the housing project, or indeed, in the black community generally. That theme is a recurring one in this book. But I do deny that there is any need for any controlling body to beat, brutally beat sick alcoholics for the crime of using scrap timber for firewood to keep warm. I do deny that there is any need for any group to become a veritable black gestapo, a brutal, arrogant jackbooting 'we'll show the whites there'll be no nonsense tolerated here' terror gang. There is a danger in giving indiscriminate power to the wrong blacks, blacks who have lost their black values. Aborigines remember well how it was the native police in early colonial history who were used as the most effective oppressors and killers of other blacks.

The first target in the clean-up campaign was, of course, the goomies. Sure, they offered violence, but I've heard over and over again from blacks in the area how the committee provoked it. Anyway, as the lowest underdogs, the gooms became the target first. Then the unmarried mothers. Also three harmless but irritating homosexuals. The Action Committee started the clean-up campaign by raiding the gooms and tipping out their metho. This happened several times. Now these blacks know quite well that alcoholics who are as far gone as these gooms are cannot be deprived of their grog because they will, in a very short time, go into acute withdrawal agony. If the metho is taken away, they need an equally cheap replacement. At first, none was provided. Later it was, because some members of the Action Committee got enterprising. They bought flagons of plonk at around $2.50 a toss and flogged them to the metho-deprived gooms during the Easter public holidays for between $4 and $5 a flagon. Not just gooms, either. Sundry other blacks availed themselves of the service because it was easier to go there than to the white-run sly-grog shop in the area. The proceeds from the sale of the booze were supposed to go into a fund. Whether it actually did is anybody's guess.

Subsequently, blacks complained that the Action Committee was walking into their houses (i.e. the houses that had not yet been done up but were being lived in) without permission. There were several more cases of bashings and at least one allegation of sexual assault. The brutality had degenerated below all reasonable standards of normal control. Several blacks rang me, in Taree, to ask whether I could stop it. Some said that messages also went to Victorian and Queensland blacks asking them to stop the terror in Redfern. Meanwhile the ones that the housing project had originally been intended for, the gooms, the homeless, the destitute, the poor bastards, were leaving. Leaving to go back to that park bench where they came from. There were originally between twenty-five and forty gooms. As I write this there's only about seven left. The rest left because they understand the persecution of white coppers but couldn't take it when the black police turned against them in exactly the same way.

By mid-June, complaints about the Action Committee and the subversion of the original aims of the project were raining in on Gordon Bryant thick and fast. His exasperation was becoming obvious and some blacks were becoming worried that he would change his mind about the grant. Not that the blacks had got their hands on any of the money yet, anyway, because a legally constituted body able to receive and be responsible for it had not yet been formed. The Aboriginal Legal Service solicitor advising the blacks, Eddy Neumann, had warned that it would be extremely difficult to form a cooperative because there would be resistance to this on what, he said, boiled down to essentially racist grounds. So it was best to form a company and elect a board of directors to run the housing project. This had so far not been achieved because of constant dissension between the originators of the project and the 'better blacks'.

I chaired the meeting at Murawina which set up the board of directors to whom Mr Bryant would be able to hand the money. Eddy Neumann told me later in the evening that compared to previous meetings, this one was the most constructive he had attended. Perhaps it was, but it was nevertheless an appalling shemozzle. It was a direct confrontation between the originators and their supporters and the 'better blacks'. Many of the Aboriginals in the room were not properly aware of the implications of what they were voting for. Eddy Neumann's explanation of why a company had to be formed was understood by few. Even less followed his comments about the law governing incorporation.

My point is, why do our people have to be subjected to this sort of thing? Why do they have to structure themselves in ways laid down by a white man's law to get a white man's handout when they should have access to compensation funds, not cap-in-hand but as a right? I know, of course, that they won't get the grant money unless they do so structure themselves. Also, they need to follow the requirements of the white man's law in this, as in other cases, in order to *protect* themselves from the white man. So you see them buggarising around trying to comprehend and do the right thing. You see them trying to meet the white boss's everlasting stipulations and requirements and you ask yourself, *why*?

Why should they have to run their lives on a white man's terms? Why should they have to grapple with the intricacies of legal requirements, rules of debate, accountancy and all the other clap-trap before such time as they have raised a generation of sons who can do it for them? Why shouldn't they have a properly set up, black-administered, black-directed National Aboriginal Development Commission, outside the public service, to do it for them? A black commission that is structurally immune from any white-anting? That could be handling all the legal requirements and funding black projects from compensation money? That could be hiring white advisers who would not be in control but who would be *directed* according to black self-determination? Would such a commission not be more realistic (provided always that it were only staffed by Aboriginal patriots) than the chaos of meetings such as the one I attended, where three quarters of the voters, only partially comprehending, were therefore flippant, irresponsible voters? You see it happen time after time in black organisations as a result. You get the stupid election of people who, capability-wise and character-wise, are generally a disaster.

The meeting provided an interesting study of the effect of the erosion of black men by white values. Thanks to Gordon Bryant and others in Canberra, Cope, Hills and the South Sydney Council failed in their primary aim — to stop the housing project. But now, the originators of the project pleaded, were Cope and Co. to achieve their 'second best aim' — the subversion of the housing project *into a black show in the white image*? Another white-dominated, white value-oriented, black-repressing edifice of sour grapes? With the loyal help of weak, self-interested blacks, was this to be the fate of the housing project?

'No,' retorted the 'better blacks'. 'A lot of needy families came along earlier to Bob Bellear for help and were turned away because he is sticking up for the gooms! Kick *them* out for they are not worth helping.' The originators retorted that 'those families weren't as needy. Most of them have homes, have some income. We've got to concentrate on the bottom rung, not end up housing well-paid blacks (who are often on a pension lurk as well) for around $8 per week.' The 'better blacks' came along with the general idea that 'I've worked hard for what I've got. I've stayed decent all my life. Why should *those* people get the benefits instead of us battlers?'

And so it went on. A lot of the 'better blacks'' arguments ran in the classic conservative vein which, examined closely, is essentially a rationalisation of greed, of selfishness. Certainly the 'better blacks' have their share of human greed. But there is more to it than this. They *do* want to show the white man. I believe that very few of the blacks who speak in the conservative manner and who espouse 'decency' in the white man's terms are aware of how they have been got at. The handful of canny, cynical opportunists aside, most blacks are unaware of the structure of the process by means of which they are being used to sell out their own. Because their identity and their black values have been eroded, they are an easy tool for the anti-black interests or even for the sympathetic paternalists who themselves do not realise how their own white middle class values are subverting true black interests. In a way the 'better blacks' are innocents and they are innocents who are quite convinced of the correctness of their stand. Yet they have been white-anted. Essentially this has been possible because they are not Aboriginal patriots. They might very well be 'decent' people, 'respectable' people — but they are *not* splendid people. They are *not* Aboriginal patriots. They are not the Aboriginal patriots who are capable of understanding why it is that the tribe is more important than the individual.

At one meeting that I attended in June, Gordon Bryant said that in his view, the housing project should have a sprinkling of what I call 'better blacks' to provide an example for the others. This is a typical viewpoint which arises out of Bryant's own set of white values. It makes sense to him and it is an understandable attitude. It is also a sad fact that this sort of thing has never worked, will never work for much the same reason that similar examples set by white men have never worked. The whole thing is regarded by blacks merely as the latest government-inspired 'assimilation' dodge.

If I want to raise a black man to a new standard, then first of all *I have to go down to where he is.* I must meet him there. I must work with him at the level he is at. If I don't do that, then in his eyes I am 'flash'; I am trying to be an 'imitation white man'. Once he thinks that of me, all he will do is resist me. *That* is why blacks aren't inspired by Neville Bonner. That is why all the 'Uncle Toms' in the movement are hated so much — they are all pushing white values for their own profit and all the blacks know it. That is why if there is to be any real growth for the people, Aboriginal patriots who can withstand the pressures of white opinions are so absolutely vital. And that is why, in his attempts to deal with blacks, a well-meaning, tolerant man such as Gordon Bryant is as much a victim of his own white man's values as black people have always been.

If I knew of a place where blacks could go to heal themselves and build a new life — a kind of black Israel which needed to be developed for blacks by blacks, I must point out that I would ask both Bob Bellear and Dick Blair to contribute. Bob for his heart, his understanding, his compassion, Dick for his strength, for all are vital ingredients of any community development project. At the moment, Dick is *not* strong, as a black man should be strong, but he could be again. We have to recognise, all of us, that we are the chained and crippled now. No matter what the South Sydney Council may think or want, the development should be catering for our chained and crippled people, not bringing more oppression upon them. When the blacks lost their Dreaming, they also lost their guidelines. Before Dick Blair can control a people he has first to control himself and then his Action Committee — for these are the ones who can bring all Aboriginal hopes to nought. Beyond this, he can strive to develop both them and himself to the standard of an Aboriginal patriot. We need so very, very many of them. For it is only through their actions, in integrity, their fidelity to a dream, that the Aboriginal race can live again.

Perhaps I should explain to the reader, in more depth, yet another reason why blacks are so easily got at, why they are so keen to forget about their origins. I have touched on it before. It is a reason beyond those of uncertain identity and unstable values which explains why blacks are so keen to become 'better blacks'. That reason is simply the memory of horror. Take, as an example, what I saw the other night. I went onto a reserve to offer a couple of mattresses to a woman who literally has nothing. She and her kids sleep on old blankets and rugs on the floor.

There is a paraplegic visiting her when I arrive — a woman. Dead from the waist down, she makes a puddle of urine under her wheelchair during the half-hour that I am there. She is unaware of what is occurring. She wants to return to her own house but can't do so without help. Suddenly you realise that the various visitors have drifted out. A drunk has come in and now huddles on a rug in the corner. You set out to find the fellow she asks you to fetch. He will help her home. When you find him, he is crying. His girlfriend has just been picked up by police on five charges and for breaking parole. You return him to the house where the cripple is waiting and he helps her out the door, still crying.

You are about to leave when another woman drifts in. She is drunk and upset because fifteen of the reserve children are due to appear in court tomorrow, charged with neglect. Five of them are hers. Her answer to it, this night as on all other nights is to get rotten, crying drunk. You take her back to her home to find that another black, a visitor there, is about to get 'rolled' because he has some grog money on him. You prevent this and send him on his way. You now make another attempt to leave. It is 1 a.m. As you get into your car someone in the house calls you to 'have a look at this'. 'This' is another drunk who, quite unconcerned about himself, has an appalling amount of blood dripping from the back of his head and onto his shirt front. Someone mumbles that, 'He fell.' The blood has already started to congeal and thick globs of it drip crazily on the floor. Six small children are peering around the door of the bedroom, giggling. At the casualty department of the local hospital, a loudly disapproving medical staff insert half a dozen stitches in the drunk's head. The sister is not amused when he advises her to 'speak proper English' and later tries to put his hand up her skirt. While she is getting his particulars, she sarcastically wants to know why he is on an invalid pension. 'How did you get on that?' He got it because he *is* an invalid, lady, to a degree that you will probably never understand.

Stitched up, you return the drunk to his house and leave to go and clean the blood out of your car. These are the things that constitute the reality of the reserves, these are the things that make up the complex of horror, the memory of horror, that the 'better blacks' are trying to forget. This is what I get my nose rubbed in when all I intended to do was offer a poor woman a couple of mattresses. It's a fine cure for the armchair view that anyone who doesn't actually live on the reserves so quickly develops.

Next day you return to the reserve for another purpose. While you are talking to one woman in front of her house, a police car cruises up. The tension heightens. The woman asks, 'I wonder who they're after this time?' It turns out that they are looking for her daughter — 'Where is she?' Emotionally she can't handle it. She can't respond reasonably, logically. So she just screams at the copper, 'Why don't you leave us alone? You've already got one of my kids. Now you're after the other. Bloody white bastards … never leave us alone. One day I'll rip all their guts out.'

The following day this same woman tells me how she and a bunch of other Aborigines and their kids, utterly crushed, were awaiting their turn before the magistrate in the morning. For some reason unknown to them and departing from usual procedure, the police that morning had made all the blacks sit together and kept them under surveillance, saying, perhaps jokingly, teasingly, 'Have any of you got any guns or hand grenades with you today?' Of course the answer was 'no'. It makes me think of the many whites who sneer at the ridiculous idea of a tiny black minority confronting twelve million white Australians. Ha, ha. But such is the desperation and the ongoing horror in the lives of these blacks that I, for one, can see the day when the answer to the coppers' question will no longer be 'no'. Instead, the answer will blow up in their superior, smiling, land-stealing, people-destroying faces.

A long-standing answer to the problem posed by the ruined human beings that I have described is to ignore them and let the canker grow. Another view says 'throw out the Aboriginal Welfare Department and send in the Red Cross'. Almost all white Australians who care at all about the problem take a 'help them, guide them, show them the way' view. Almost nobody can get his mind around what blacks really want — land, compensation, discreet non-dictatorial help and *to be left alone* by white Australia. You'll never heal a wound if you keep on picking at it.

Mr Bryant, remember when you said, 'none of us know the answers to social questions, whether people are black or white'? You are probably right. But some people are a little nearer the answers than others and these are the ones who always get it in the neck because they won't fight quite so dirty, quite so hypocritically. I know that a lot of blacks are artful dodgers. I know they would try the patience of a saint. I know that you've got to be a veritable Solomon to even begin to handle Aboriginal affairs properly. But I also know that there is a fine line of truth in all these things — a line that can be found and walked upon — which is the message of this book.

There is a danger that when the black compensation claim starts being pushed seriously, the government will say, 'Hey, hold on a minute … You've got half a million dollars in Redfern, so much here, so much there. *That's* your compensation.' Here lie the seeds for the conflict of tomorrow. For no grassroots black is ever going to regard *any* hideously expensive, white-anted, white-controlled showpiece, no matter how much it costs, as anything but the travesty that in truth it is. *When* will white men ever realise that it is no use giving the substance unless they also give the spirit? Any grant, any development is *not* going to be regarded as compensation in direct proportion to the degree of direct or indirect white-anting that it has suffered. It becomes mere palliation. Real compensation will only be paid in so far as the money sets up a situation which allows for real human growth for blacks.

Labor in power is the best thing that has happened to blacks for a long time. Gordon Bryant has demonstrably done more for Aborigines in a short time than any of his predecessors. I've seen him cop rotten, barbed criticism and come up smiling. He has shown elasticity and tolerance. He has a rotten, lonely job and is in the near impossible situation of being part of a Labor caucus composed of only a small handful of pro-black sympathisers, an opposing group that is actively anti-black and a majority who couldn't care less one way or another (provided it doesn't cost too much). These things are probably part of the reason why the first fine flush, the original impetus, has slowed down now. I bet Bryant is going to have money troubles before too much longer, too.

At this stage, I can only judge Gordon Bryant from the impressions that I have formed from watching him on three occasions. Beyond that, I don't know what he is like, cannot yet read his soul or evaluate his motivations (especially as I'm not interested in other people's opinions of him). But I do know that Labor is hampered by the same tired old assumptions that have characterised all Aboriginal administrations in the past. That is, 'we'll lean down, stretch out the hand of brotherhood and help you poor blacks, do for you poor blacks'. Do you understand why white interference, white administration is never going to work? Do you see why blacks are so sceptical about whites who are supposed to be interested in their cause? Do you see,

Mr Bryant, why your old dream of getting to where you could *really* do something at last is going to be proved to be so much ratshit? Do you see why self-determination that isn't really real *is* so much ratshit? Do you see why a white man'll *never* do it? And it's *not* because of black obstinacy, black uselessness, unreason or ingratitude. It's not 'because you can't really help them'. The hatred continues because, in the final analysis, *you will not* give it in the way that the black man can use it. You appear to be a reasonable man. So let us reason together, you the white man and us blacks, before the sterile norms of white/black relations once again reassert themselves.

I have heard, through the grapevine, that I upset Dick Hall on the occasion that we met at a public meeting because I accused him of subverting the Aboriginal Housing Project. Now I've nothing against Dick Hall. I don't know him and before that weekend I didn't even know of him. He might very well be an excellent PR man and a fine minister's Mr Fix-It. He might, by his own lights, be doing a genuine job. But nevertheless, like so many whites before him, he has been brought into a new field to become an instant expert (as all whites seem to become as soon as they enter Aboriginal affairs). When are we finally going to learn that Aboriginal affairs doesn't need any more highly qualified white whiz kids?

It seems to be always my fate to end up getting offside with politicians and officials. Is it because I get to the emotional truth of things? Is it because I point out embarrassing things like how it appears that there is some sort of enormous, elaborate game being played in Aboriginal affairs? The aim of the game seems not to be the advancement of the black mass but the advancement of ambitious individuals of both races. And I'll bet that even a reform-minded minister is only partially able to control this, especially as, given the trap of his own white values, he will sooner or later become part of the game. It mightn't be a popular thing to say but nevertheless, if blacks are really to advance, they must be rid of the growing army of gubbahs who, having lucrative, comfortable jobs in Aboriginal affairs, generally paying upwards of $10,000 to $15,000 or more a year, will let the said jobs go over their dead bodies. (Thank God for the Aboriginal problem!) We all know why it is that public service authoritarianism and the unspoken public service ethic, 'It's not what's done that matters. It's what *appears* to be done; that's what counts,' will never advance blacks. Blacks have never been fooled by it. There's no chance for growth in it. Blacks *must* strive for a higher standard than the 'if it *looks* good it *is* good' attitude. They *must* rise above the general Australian 'I'm alright Jack, buggar you' folk ethic.

We must have black Israels — places where Aboriginal patriots can help to heal their crippled race as well as themselves. Places where clean, black people with firm values will be able to set up alcoholic aid centres, hospitals and rehabilitation projects. Where blacks will help their brothers rediscover the secret, hidden joys of the spirit known to their ancestors — free of all accretions of dogma. There must be rest and treatment centres for the emotionally crippled, the blacks whose nerves have been bombed out.

I do not reject public servants, as human beings. Nor do I reject their skills. Many of them would be most useful in a black Israel, helping blacks, teaching blacks. They would undoubtedly be able to use their skills to better effect than they can in the public service. But I do reject the idea that they should be in charge of things, or indeed, that any white man should ever run a black Israel. (The white man who could do so successfully would be a most unique human being; one of the rare breed whose humanity transcends his colour.) I do not reject the conservative or 'better blacks' either. They do have standards that are worth incorporating into a black Israel. But first they must become black men and women again. Many of them, reading this book or this chapter are going to deny that what I have written is correct. 'He didn't really know what was going on there' or 'he doesn't know the full story of this' they'll say. But in their hearts they're going to know what I am getting at. They're going to know it as surely as they keep in their guts the memory of that horror back on the mission. Perhaps some will have the grace, at least to themselves, to admit shame.

When I go onto the reserve, blacks sometimes say to me, 'But you can help us. You are supposed to be a leader. You know the answers.' In fact, I cannot help. I cannot even begin to help. Nor can I help the children as these cripples perpetuate their kind from generation to generation. Nor can the white man do anything about it. Only massive, imaginative, non-obtrusive, black-directed government funding can allow me, and others like me, to begin to help them. And once we start to do this, then we will also be able to help the 'decent' blacks, those who have turned away from their own in a reaction from horror, those who have, in their own way, become as solidly a part of the Aboriginal problem as any reserve drunk can ever be.

*

So ended the original version of this chapter, covering events up until late June. Things looked pretty bad — almost a complete rout of foundation ideas about the aims and functions of the housing project. However, black community opinion in Redfern was swinging increasingly behind those who felt that the project should adhere to these foundation ideals. At the meeting with Gordon Bryant in June, I had suggested that a paid black administrator be employed to run the housing project and be responsible to the board of directors. Many people were worried when Aub Phillips, Dick Blair's brother, was elected to the job at the 'shemozzle' meeting. However, I have since been told by blacks that Aub has shown himself to be a capable and sincere administrator. There are plenty of fights to be fought yet over the housing project but with Redfern blacks becoming more aware of the importance of helping those most in need in their own community, it is now starting to look as if the project will achieve something worthwhile after all. Overt white interference in the affairs of the project has stopped, thanks probably to Gordon Bryant. The Action Committee's activity has also ceased — some blacks say that it doesn't exist any more. The gooms are slowly, hesitatingly returning to the project — limping back from the prisons and the park benches. There are fifteen there now.

Bob and Kaye are also back and Kaye is nursing her goomies again. She may soon receive a small wage from the Aboriginal Medical Service for her efforts.

Yes, at the moment things look hopeful. But people's self-interest is an all-pervading thing and human nature being what it is, I don't doubt that it won't be too long before a new crop of 'better blacks' will be trying to get onto a cheap rent lurk. In Aboriginal affairs too, you often see a curious blurring of the 'goodies' and the 'baddies' according to circumstance, expediency and self-interest (whether that interest is serving the demands of materialism or of the ego). This blurring occurs because very few blacks are solid either in their Aboriginality or in their loyalties. There is no Aboriginal cultural identity as such, no set of firm black standards to live by. The only real link these people have is their black skin, their poverty and their shared experiences of persecution and of horror.

I do not doubt that I could rewrite this chapter again in another four weeks. If things have changed again it will be because the Redfern Aboriginal Housing Project is built on the shifting sands of conflicting, petty egos. If it were built on the backs of Aboriginal patriots it would stand like a rock. At the risk of being tedious, I must say it again. Until we have such patriots, each toss of the dice will bring a new chaos, a new confusion. It is such confusion that ensures that it is impossible to predict how the Aboriginal Housing Project will shape. Won't it be interesting, though, to see who's got it in, say, two years' time?

15

Towards a New Black Man

GRANNY KOORI

Dear Director of Aboriginal Grants
My association needs $55,000 bucks
To purchase silky black ladies pants
A quota to cover each area, the Territories —
State by state
To conceal from the prying eyes of the world
The Aborigines poor buggared fate.
There's few men with ESSENTIALS among 'em
We think lots of bloomers will meet
Requirements of dress as befits them
While women fight for black kids on the street!
Blackblokes think they're great 'lovers' and 'manly'
A MAN 'cause he drinks lots of grog
They leave it to women to battle
Far as 'love' goes — so does my dog!!
A REAL man stops children from dyin'
A REAL man don't belt up his gin
A REAL man don't grog away money
To let wolves of hunger come in
A REAL man in old tribal custom
Held to the law and its way

He didn't starve kids — or his missus
Not like the weak blacks of today!
So expedite bloomers — first mail please
We've hoped for too long they'll be MEN
Now we'll cover their doongles with panties —
And start out all over again!!!

GRANDFATHER KOORI

Now Granny get yer fanny
Out of here, I'll have MY say
'Course the blacks are kinda useless
Since the whites come here to stay.
With 200 years of bribin', baccy flour grog an tea
Each has made its mighty inroads on a people who were free
But they're NOT the 'free' no longer, they're the Chained and crippled now
And it takes a lot of courage for a man to face his hour.
Sure, the women march for justice while near all the men stay home
But there's a small few men there with you — little bricks are building Rome
Solid bricks and solid women with love's cement in their hand
Will block and build a nation — once they've won their bit of land
Once we've won our bit of land back we'll put bludgers to the rout
And we'll fight and form an empire — further out, much further out.

Blacks as a separate entity are going to increase despite all the assimilation policies and wishful thinking about a homogenous society. The influence of a new black consciousness is going to militate more and more against part-Aboriginal people, however pale, dropping out into white society. While conservatives tend to rubbish anything that is traditionally Aboriginal, a more wholesome instinct is manifesting itself in the young blacks who are taking tentative steps to go back, to revive the knowledge of things traditional and to promote them as something for blacks to feel proud about. As Paul Coe said,

> We're trying to invite tribal people to come to Sydney to teach young kids. Even if they don't teach us the culture of our particular tribes, at least we'll be able to learn aspects of the Aboriginal culture from certain other tribes — which will be invaluable.

Hand in hand with attempts to foster a positive black consciousness, hopefully, will be curriculum changes in Australian schools and the gradual phasing out of text-books that show racist bias against Aborigines. If healthier attitudes about race were taught to young Australians everywhere then, given time, perhaps our schools would not be quite the ghastly experiences they are now for so many young Aborigines.

'Assimilation', as promoted by various governments over the years, has involved a deliberate policy of sprinkling blacks amongst white neighbours, the idea being that this will stimulate a black family into shaping up in white terms and help them to lose their black identity gradually. It is argued that wherever blacks settle as a group, they will only form 'another mission' with all the horrors that *that* connotes. Many blacks agree with this policy, because they have never seen an all-black group with any type of internal discipline and do not believe that it can come. Other blacks, again, say it can. I personally believe that it can only come in highly specialised circumstances, in black Israels which I have described elsewhere.

Wherever you look, it is obvious that blacks never have, and never will, respond to a white man's rule. All it has created is crippling, a handout mentality which is the very devil and a mute resistance that hides a volcano of hate. Queensland has 'assisted' black people for years — to no avail! Even blacks that are completely crushed, of no use to themselves or anyone else, are saying, 'Let us do it ourselves. Let us make our own decisions. Sure, we'll make mistakes, but let us have a go.'

In part, at least, the Labor Party seems to have got the message. At Newcastle, in reply to a question about the self-direction of blacks Gordon Bryant said,

> I think you start with simple things. They make some decision for themselves which actually produces a result. That is, they decide they want their toilet shifted. Then you say 'Where to?' They work it out and it happens. That's just a very elementary thing. But my impression is that they have never been able to make decisions and see anything come of it. And so I think that my job is to create a situation where the decision-making process is largely Aboriginal and when they've made a decision, something happens as a result of it.

Right on, and at a local level self-determination must start off with things as simple as this. However, blacks have been urging for years that it must be so at the *other end* of the spectrum too, i.e. that there must be black *policy-making* bodies, not just advisory or consultative committees that have no policy-making power or only partial policy-making power. Aborigines haven't achieved that yet. And remember that the most influential of the various groups that advise on Aboriginal policy, the Council for Aboriginal Affairs, is an all-white body. Certainly its three white members are recognised as experts on Aboriginal affairs and have a distinguished record of sympathy to the black cause. But I'll stand stuffing if any of the three can ever even *begin* to give voice to the aspirations of the Aboriginal people.

On the other hand, Bryant did say in a press release on February 1, 1973 that, besides his proposals for a 100 man Aboriginal field force of liaison officers, it was also necessary to have a larger number of Aborigines in the career structure of the Department of Aboriginal Affairs and he stressed that he *envisaged a basically Aboriginal Department in ten years' time.*

Apparently this was a bit much from a Departmental point of view, for three weeks later Aboriginal Affairs Director Barry Dexter was quoted in *The Sydney Morning Herald* (24/2/73) as saying that he had just put a proposal to appoint Aborigines to work beside senior officers in the Department of Aboriginal Affairs to the Public Service Board. Eventually hundreds of blacks would be employed, he said, 'although he hoped it would never become a black Department. There will always be a need for some whites in all areas.' Mr Dexter doesn't say so outright, but the context suggests that these whites would hardly be in subordinate positions.

What does Dexter's Aboriginal member of staff Charles Perkins think of this point of view? Says he:

> I don't think anything will ever be of serious consequence in Aboriginal affairs until Aborigines run their own affairs. White people can have the best motivation, but [still] they're white people. We remain Aborigines … we live it — whites can only dabble in it. I don't care what else happens. But what *has* to happen is that Aborigines have to run Aboriginal affairs. They've got to be the people who make the policy, implement it, right from the top down to the bottom, as much as possible. Some fields we can't cover right at the time, such as accountancy and other such specialised fields, but we can still pay people to do this, white people. Provided we tell them what to do.

So there it is, total disagreement. Some blacks might feel that isolation will be bad for the movement, which has elements of truth in it too. Yet I do feel that potential black growth is only possible in the terms Perkins has stated — black control, allied with white help. I believe this, no matter how hopeless and ill-directed the black control may initially be.

Bobbi Sykes put her finger on the thing at issue here:

> Having made sure, in the past, that blacks didn't get educated and that many of them did suffer from brain

> damage, that therefore their comprehension is, in some cases, completely ruined, whites will say 'we'll illustrate that blacks can't do it. We'll get a group of people who have no expertise other than that they're black (and whom we've already fucked up in the past) and they'll soon *prove* that blacks can't do it. After which we'll put in our *own* experts.' ... In the area in which we are trying to do something — in the area of a national lobby — we *have no* expertise! We have blacks! We've got plenty of blacks. We've got blacks who are willing, blacks who would break their *backs* — but we don't have blacks with the know-how ... and so far, we don't have access to expertise. And I think that the government and the people of Australia will be standing by waiting for the blacks to make *just one mistake*. There's such a concentration of racist publicity on the whole thing ... I think that with those sort of pressures on the blacks ... there can be no freedom to make mistakes, or experiment to find out which is the right way, especially since you've been kept from making these experiments in the past.

White paternalism, even benevolent paternalism, will, at this point be taking a wise, pensive puff at its cigar and saying to Bobbi and young blacks like her, 'Dere, dere girl, you *must* be patient. Rome wasn't built in a day ... you must wait, girl, wait ...' which, of course, will herald another generation of blacks *being done to*. Indian readers contemplating Bobbi's complaint may perhaps cast their minds back to the time before independence, when they were solemnly assured that the country would run to the pack without British rule, that the mistakes that would be made would be horrendous. Somehow, India survived it and there hasn't been any signs since that its people contemplate calling the British Raj back in.

Whether, in white minds, it is reasonable or not, more and more blacks are rejecting all forms of white control and are rejecting the assimilationist ideas that demand that they give up a separate black consciousness. The most extreme form of alienation is expressed in the demand for a separate state for blacks. 'Libertas', quoted in Chapter 4, recommended that on account of how blacks are dirty, lazy, obscene, etc., black people and white people ought to live in separate communities. By a vastly different process of reasoning, blacks like Paul Coe come to the same conclusion:

> The separate state idea flows naturally from the fact that we've *always* been separated from the white community. We've never been a part of the white Australian mainstream of life. Every time we've tried to join it, we've been shunted off. The only way we could join it is by becoming imitation white men. And I think that if a man has to almost prostitute himself in order to join something, he's better off without joining and by maintaining his own separate identity. The people should be in a position to make and implement their own laws and live by them, rather than have other laws forced upon them. Blacks have always been separated. I think this should be acknowledged. The Aboriginal Australian is NOT a part of the European–Australian culture but is a part of a Third World culture — always has been. The separate state idea is not new. It's just taken them a while to actually formulate it into words. But the basic feeling of separation has always been there. I think the reserves typify this. On a reserve, people get some feelings of security — from each other. It's only when they come into the white community that they suffer oppression and hatred.
>
> I don't believe that the federal government is really sincere and I don't believe that it is prepared to make any fundamental changes ... They've been in power now for four months but they haven't done anything. Gordon Bryant *knows* the problems. Yet he's been tripping about the country! I can't see any reason why he cannot put into the field, *now,* massive medical and nutritional teams to stop the infants dying. I cannot see why they cannot

put into the field *now* — on the same scale that they put people into the Vietnam war, the same scale, the same expenditure of money — teams to stop the black infant mortality rate, teams to make people understand the powers they could have if they used the legal services properly. And I see no reason why the federal government cannot grant land rights now, do all these things *now*.

[Some blacks say 'work through the system'] but I don't think there will ever be a true Aboriginal voice while we've got to rely on a white parliamentary system ... because while we are in a minority and they are in a majority, we'll *always* be at a disadvantage, a group given tokens, simply by definition of the fact that we are prepared to exist and work within *their* structures. The only time an Aboriginal man or woman will get a true voice is when they've got their *own* institutions and are self-governing ...

The world is changing rapidly ... the white man all around the world has been taught to realise that he no longer controls this world, that he no longer has the arrogance to walk around the world as if it's his own. The black man is starting to realise that he has an equal share in this world. The yellow man is starting to realise that, too. Most enlightened blacks, at least in revolutionary groups, regard Australia as one of the last bastions of white supremacy. And all the people I spoke to in the States — blacks — said that when the movement is finished in Africa, because that's their first priority, Australia would be the next one on their list. And I don't believe that the Aboriginal people have yet learned to understand the power that they have at their disposal. They have tremendous potential power internationally — not so much internally, but they have great power internationally. This is something that they've got at their disposal which the Australian government has not got. I think if they start to learn to utilise this power properly, they can one day ensure that they bring about an Aboriginal state — a separate state where Aboriginal people are in full control ... with *their* laws deciding

> which way they govern themselves, how they live etc. To me it's quite feasible, in the next ten to fifteen or twenty years to see this development come about and probably much sooner.

Such are a young man's dreams. Leaving out all the other considerations that spring to mind, it seems to me that defence and security considerations alone will ensure that the black separate state that Paul wants (The Northern Territory) will remain a dream. And yes, I know that blacks dream of a world-wide united black movement that is going to sweep the iniquitous white man off his throne wherever he reigns, but I don't believe it. No African nation, or nations, beset by internal problems, tribal rivalries, balance of payments difficulties, trade agreements, religious and social factions and all the rest of it are going, at any time in the foreseeable future, to set sail for the antipodes to save Australian blacks just because they are black. Nor will they shovel in finance by the ton. It's just not on. It reminds me of something Bob Maa said that he noticed on his American trip; the Negro students were interested enough in hearing about Aboriginal problems, but the older Negroes were too involved with their own problems to give a hang about Aboriginal issues. It's one thing for American Negroes to say nice things to a black visitor from Australia at a time when good feelings run high. It's quite another thing to get meaningful aid over and above the 'let's exchange delegates each year' level, especially from people who have as much on their plates as Negroes in the USA have. It seems to me that the best profit Aborigines can make of other blacks in other countries is in the sphere of opinion-making. If African and Asian nations can be educated to vote against Australia in the United Nations on issues of unfair treatment of Aborigines, it will be one more contribution to the formation of a climate of world opinion on the subject. And this, Paul himself well knows.

The Labor government has not yet, except in an ad hoc, fragmentary fashion, shown up on either of the two most important aspects of the Aboriginal claim — land and compensation. Each is useless without the other; they *must* be complementary. There is no definite policy about compensation at all, as far as I can see. Point 5 of the federal Labor policy on Aborigines states somewhat vaguely that, in compensation for traditional lands, funds will be made available to assist Aborigines who wish to purchase their own homes. A perfect 'Catch 22'! At Newcastle, Mr Bryant was asked about the land issue and the issue of compensation for blacks to allow them to re-establish themselves on that land. Pointing out that he didn't want to preempt anything that Judge Woodward might say, he added that, of course, land had already been granted in a number of areas. But, he went on,

> Then you come to the Aboriginal people in Sydney who for a century haven't had any land of their own. What you do about that, I don't know. I'm not keen on paying cash contributions to anybody. I *am* prepared to sponsor something by which people get some special advantages, something like the repatriation system where people get continuing benefits such as medical services, housing, education, etc. throughout their life-time ... I won't support, at this stage anyhow, any system whereby say, you get a cheque for $20,000.

The Aboriginal land claim supports this latter idea; there is absolutely no point in giving compensation to individuals in the condition they are in at the moment. You might as well throw the money away, for all the good it would do. Hence the call for a trust fund. Special advantages would, of course, help a lot of Aborigines, the same as they would underprivileged whites. But the unique point of the land/compensation claim is that it allows Aborigines to *re-establish themselves* as full human beings, to give them some chance to heal. Repatriation style benefits will *never* do this, any more than any other handouts have ever done.

Hand in hand with the land/compensation claim is the call for Aboriginal self-determination. So that *they* may decide how compensation money is to be spent to develop *their* land. So that *they* may decide what type of white professionals shall be engaged to help them. I notice that white Australia is far less against the idea of separate development (as distinct from apartheid) than it used to be. Said the Minister for Aboriginal Affairs at Newcastle:

> As far as I'm concerned, I can see no reason why a community, of which there are some thirty or forty in the Northern Territory and another sixty or seventy scattered throughout the rest of Australia [It's more than that, Gordon; New South Wales alone has, is it forty-one reserves, not to speak of non-reserve places of long-standing Aboriginal use such as Weilmoringle ... Why, oh why can't you whites learn that it is not only the full-blood tribal people that are Aborigines?] which are basically Aboriginal in context, shouldn't be judged as other Australian towns ... Take Arnhem Land for instance. There's about 4500 to 5000 people there and they're in half a dozen reasonably large communities ... I cannot see any reason why they shouldn't just develop that way. They are a part of Australia and they come and go as they wish and they govern their own affairs. It was pointed out to me earlier today that that's exactly what the Navajo Indians do. I haven't got any feelings for or against it. If people want to live in one spot, amongst themselves, that suits me alright.

The land claim calls for reserves, traditional sites and sites of sacred significance and *extra* areas in each state, preferably in one piece. I believe that on some of the Indian reserves in Canada, *Indian* laws obtain. The white man's law stops at the reservation border. This situation is interesting and bears further examination because it is yet another means of establishing black independence. Black areas would cease to be open to the public. Access would not be according to the whims of some white administrator as in the past, but would be subject to a decision by a black council (with special conditions governing the access of police chasing criminals).

That, in outline, is what black Australia requires of the white man (subject, of course, to verification and discussion by a nationally convened, for the first time ever, properly representative, unrigged conference of blacks). The Aboriginal nation, as a nation of the spirit, a nation without a flag, a nation without land or hope, a nation of underprivilege, has existed, probably, from about a generation after Captain Cook landed. Occasionally you meet one of its patriots, one of those people, who, whatever their intermediate likes and loyalties, can be seen to cast their ultimate sympathy, the core of their feelings with this Aboriginal nation. Ultimately too, I have noticed that there is always another idea concurrent with the concept of an Aboriginal patriot and implicit in it — the idea of an integrated, undivided human being — a whole person of whatever colour. In the two above senses, one does not meet many Aboriginal patriots because it takes a special kind of vision to be one. And it takes courage. I would say that Pearl Gibbs is one. I've never met the man, but he sounds like one — Jacob Oberdoo. Bill Harney was one. I think that Bob Bellear might be one. There are undoubtedly some others. I bet Kath Walker could name me some. Daisy Bindi? Bill Ferguson?

The list is not a big one. Many names are conspicuously absent. But you figure it out. *Were* they Aboriginal patriots, those undisciplined glory hunters who siphoned off Aboriginal Breakfast Programme moneys and Embassy funds to pay for their bit of slap 'n tickle in high class motels? Who take people's money and are never able to show with anything real, anything concrete, what they have done with it? *Were* they Aboriginal patriots who managed to get all the blame for kitty-tickling shunted onto one lame duck while getting clear away with it themselves? Or those who lined up their empty flagons outside the Embassy tent for a nation to laugh at? And *does* an Aboriginal patriot allow himself to be filmed, on his back, snarling and sassing an old lady, whether she be white or black, as was shown in the film *Ningla A-na*? Indeed, many are called, but few are chosen. There are not many real Aboriginal patriots although there are plenty of blacks who are not far off. The bulk of our people currently are too far down, however, to fill any role other than that of underprivilege.

If we are to build a healthy black society on our little portions, our black Israels all over this continent, we will need doctors, lawyers, engineers, agriculturists, accountants, you name it. We all know that reserve kids can't become these things. Not, anyway, unless they are taken off the mission very, very young. Because it ruins them, it poisons them — and all blacks, if they want to be honest, will admit it. The reserves are pest-holes. Trouble is, we don't want the kids *off* the reserves either, because if that happens, they don't remain black people. (It doesn't necessarily mean they are 'assimilated' either. What I mean is that they don't remain 'black people' in the way that blacks who have always lived together are.) And we don't just want doctors, lawyers, engineers, agriculturists, accountants — we want *black* doctors, *black* lawyers, *black* engineers, and so on. So what have we got to do? *Change the reserves*!

Remember Alice Briggs in Chapter 1?

> But they've ruined them and the neglect is not on the part of the Aborigine because it's a white man that's put it on 'em. He's made our men lazy, he's made our women what they are and everything that goes with it … and it all comes from a white man … And I for one don't want to see my kids grow up in the conditions that I've grown up in … as second-class human beings all their life!

Wouldn't Alice go, like a shot, to a clean new black Israel to try and cure herself and cure her family … try at least? Wouldn't she, eh? Wouldn't you, if you were Alice? If you were a woman who realised that your whole life had, somehow, missed having any point? Wouldn't you like to have a go, even if your body wasn't real healthy and you had a lot wrong with you?

And Audrey, from another reserve. She is slightly retarded from malnutrition as a kid. She is barely literate, is unmarried and has two babies. She lives her life on the reserve with her parents in a tin shanty, with dirt floors, an open fireplace, no running water, no bathtub, no proper laundry facilities, no knowledge of basic hygiene, no means of self-expression. Endowment day, the occasional movie, and the odd visit from a long-standing boyfriend are the events of her life, although she is fast losing her enthusiasm for the latter because now it hurts — the beginning of a cancer of her reproductive organs.

And Charlie from the same reserve, same conditions. All his adult life spent on social services because there is no work for him. Too frail to work on the roads. Too frail to be in a football team. Not allowed into clubs, unwelcome in darts teams etc. Has long ago become an alcoholic because what else is there to do? He has seven children. His poor physique and poor diet ensure that even if he were given a job, even a light job, he won't be able to sustain it. They say that he is lazy but in Charlie's case the problem isn't laziness — it's sickness.

And so the roll-call of the raw material of the Aboriginal nation goes on. There are many Audreys, many Charlies. It is just nonsense to suggest that they can make it alone. But what Alice said is also true 'the white man'll *never* do it'. It is the stronger blacks who must help, using the tools of land rights and compensation. We've seen the shemozzle that 'leadership' causes. So let's forget leadership. Yet there's got to be *something*, because it is once again an undeniable fact that many of our people are still content to sit back and let someone else think for them, do for them. (That's why the white man flows in so often — gubbahs *abhor* a vacuum!)

It seems to me that what is needed is Aboriginal personnel who have been thoroughly trained in community organising, in how to stimulate a people into new creative channels. And there must be more than this. There must be discipline. Young men and not so young men who have never worked in their lives, who have bludged off women for years, must be given what will undoubtedly, at first, be a pretty big shock. The black community will have to decide on stern rules, tough rules that Aborigines do not like exercising against one another. Rules that say, 'Work or get out.' 'Work, or don't eat.' 'Work, or no grog.' The bludgers', the drunkards', the house neglectors', the wife and child bashers' days *must* be numbered in any developing Aboriginal community, otherwise that community will never attain any self-respect. It will never cease to be just 'another mission'. The people will have to set up committees that have enough dignity, confidence, courage and sense of discipline to exercise control. Remember back, Kooris, when our society was 'specialised' to allow for survival? When every contribution, every grain of seed, every hunt counted? When bludgers could not be afforded? So it must be again. Each community will have to appoint itself a progress committee, responsible for community control, the provision of medical aid and the multitude of other needs of a group of people. The days of tolerance for weaklings have to end. It was OK, once, to tolerate them, because job discrimination and all the rest of it made them what they were. But it can't be allowed to continue in a black Israel.

The problem on reserves and off them has always been one of inadequate motivation. Why, when there are adult men unemployed, don't you see community gardens on every reserve? Gardens that will feed everybody? Because the people have not had the motivation to create them or to continue with them. And of course the fact that they have had no security on the reserves, have been all along just 'campin' on a white feller's reserve' counts for a lot, too. It's the same thing in towns. Some white people I know have a factory in Sydney. They told me that they won't employ Aborigines any more. They're not racists. In fact, once upon a time they went out of their way to give blacks a go. They made the blacks' working conditions pleasant, too. But the nature of the production being what it is, they are very dependent on their staff being reliable. After blacks had walked out on them on three occasions, at a time when the factory could least afford to lose staff (and the blacks concerned knew it), they decided that no more Aborigines would be hired. All I could say when they told me this was, 'I don't blame you.' Yet I also knew what was behind it. Each of the three black employees had come from country areas. However nice the white employers might be, when a certain mood, a loneliness, an alienation hits many blacks from the country, they've *got* to go back to their people, to familiar territory. There's nothing you can do about it. The motivation to go back is much stronger than the motivation to stay and work. (That's why a favourite white idea that 'EDUCATION will solve all the blacks' problems' is such nonsense. Why pick up a kid, whiz him to Sydney, slap a scholarship in his hand and then wonder why he doesn't stay the distance? Isn't it better to help him *in* his community and help all the others at the same time so that he isn't put on the outer by them saying that he is 'flash'?)

But amongst their own, working for themselves and for their people, for self-sufficiency, it would be different. A different spirit would prevail. Bob Maza, on his travels through parts of Queensland and Western Australia saw all-black construction gangs in road-making, railway building, etc. Said he, of these gangs:

(a) the authorities were full of praise for their workmanship;
(b) morale was at an all-time high;
(c) there was little evidence of conflict from within;
(d) the whole thing built good strong healthy black men that no whites dared mess with.

Added Bob,

> There are undoubtedly many reasons why this should be, but I think that the greatest thing that resulted from this type of situation was the last mentioned. During my stay on the job I saw drunkards, no-hopers and social misfits moulded into shape by the encouragement, enthusiasm and sometimes reprimands of their *own* kind. Laziness was reproached, slovenliness was sweated out of them, water shyness received gang dunkings (sometimes while fully dressed) and overall they were welded into a part of one crack unit.

Gangs like these would have the same effect on their members in Aboriginal Israels. Blacks have got to make the weak elements (and there are some lulus) shape up or get out. Occasionally the shaping up process might even require the use of a solid pair of boots or a good green stick but if the committee cannot wield this authority, then the cause is lost from the start. For there is no growth in this type of weakness if it is allowed to go unchecked. By means of gangs such as Bob mentions, Aboriginal men could return to their manhood. Become once again men with status amongst their own.

And Aboriginal women, too. The sluts, the child neglectors, the irresponsibles — handled by community ostracism, 'shame' and, if necessary, a hiding from the other women. Because if little children, babies, are knocked down by cars while crossing the road unattended, then it's *not* the fault of the white man. It is squarely the fault of a lazy, neglectful, unloving mother and every black bloody well knows it. Don't tell me that a basic understanding of what children must eat to stay healthy, a basic knowledge of hygiene, can't be learnt by black women. For years, though, welfare authorities have been sending pamphlets to reserves. They give simple outlines about food values, disease, pest control, worms and so on. None of it makes a scrap of difference. It isn't even read. Worm tablets aren't even given to the children. The people just refuse to be 'done to' by whites, no matter how genuine the white man might be. But if these things were taught by example and as a process of discovery by blacks to blacks, it would be a different story. We'd *all* be learners, together.

Many Aborigines are going to squeal about my view. They are going to say, 'He's preaching *white* values!' And I'm saying, white values be fucked! It is *human* values not to neglect and starve your kids. It is *human* values to work and contribute to your own community. It is *human* values to keep your house clean. It is *human* values to stop your kids from dying. It is *human* values to maintain a level of conduct commensurate with dignity and pride. It was so in the tribe, it is so today if human development is to have any meaning.

You see dirty, lazy blacks trying to excuse themselves by saying that they refuse to keep themselves or their homes clean because they want, totally, to 'reject white values'. Who are they kidding? It would be understandable if it *were* only a reaction against the white man. But it is far more a case of dirty, lazy blacks trying to rationalise their own lack of character. Dirt has never been a virtue — in any society. If you don't believe me, if you still think that I'm preaching white values, if you want tribal authority for this view, then I invite you to consider how Dr Charles Duguid, in his recent book *Doctor and the Aborigines*, related how the nomadic Aborigines had a good sense of personal hygiene. He told of seeing a tribal Aboriginal woman holding out her baby for a bowel motion and then cleaning its buttocks by scraping them gently with a flat stone. After that she powdered them with fine sand. Dr Duguid also added that, in contrast, his wife had told him of the expression of disgust on one Aboriginal mother's face when she was staying with the Duguids and was shown how a white mother used nappies for a baby and washed them clean after use. There's your tribal authority for decent standards, for proper human values. Filth is more the symptom of a demoralised society, a symptom of the *loss* of values. So sing me no songs, you professional Aborigines cowering under the umbrella of one another's weaknesses, sing me no songs about cultural differences, cultural values, cultural excuses. We *must* be strong.

The Aboriginal committees should think also in terms of family training programmes so that blacks can learn carpentry, mechanics, dress making, timber milling, market gardening, dairying and farming and so on. White teachers and experts in marketing might be hired. Committees could be formed to foster youth activities, sports, handicrafts and aspects of traditional culture. Black land in the Riverina, the Hawkesbury area, the Darling River area and so on could produce beef, fat lambs, cotton and oilseed crops, pet foods. Entire families, not individuals, would undertake training programmes to fit them for life in the outside competitive white society or to fit them to remain and live on black land. As they produced they would earn and have the option of developing shops, homes etc. on black land or on other land that they might wish to purchase in the area.

Blacks could form experimental theatre foundations. In tourist areas perhaps Aboriginal tourist and economic development associations, funded by compensation monies and by mining royalties, could be set up to run hotel-motels, safari tours with black guides. Blacks could make part of the Great Barrier Reef a giant tourist attraction offering, perhaps, underwater railways or tunnel walks with viewing windows. Water entertainment could be provided by means of speedy plastic boats — or underwater 'big game' hunts seen through plastic hulled submarines. The developments possible in traditional Aboriginal areas such as Mootwingee and Ayers Rock are obvious. Blacks could move into the lucrative prawning industry on a large scale. Or they could start to think about … woops! The old jail dreams are getting a bit long-winded. But you see what I mean. Some areas, blacks may prefer to leave as they are. There is no doubt that this will happen too. Places left natural, where blacks can go 'to recharge their batteries'. Perhaps blacks will, at last, be given a real chance to take their place in twentieth century Australia. The level at which they do so, once they have been given the *full* chance, is up to them.

Henry Mayer in an article in *The Australian* (17/4/73), 'Atoning for a gift of poisoned flour', drew attention to the difficulty of arriving at a definitive point of atonement. Obviously Europeans are not going to leave this country, so what atonement short of *that* will do? How do you put a price on the lost self-determination of Aboriginals? Some of this book is an attempt to contribute to the debate on this aspect of atonement — what Mayer calls the 'cost/benefit approach to injustice'. Whether the Labor government will have the imagination to explore these ideas and cede justice in full measure I do not know. We must remember that $50 million dollars over a ten year period is to be allocated to the purchase of land for blacks. Yet on a point of comparative values, consider for a moment the cost of only a section of our defence equipment: twenty-four F111s at an estimated bill of $324 million. Placed beside items like this, the cost to Australia of a full measure of justice, as defined by blacks, is not such a tremendous thing after all.

Paid in full measure, it is still too much to expect that the hatred will stop, the claims will stop. I know too many blacks for whom the *hating* is the thing, the stirring is the thing, *not* what can be got from it to build with. That is what Henry Mayer was perhaps alluding to when he concluded that 'it may not be possible to find a clearcut and defensible point where you can say, with a clear conscience: "We can stop now. The job of restoration is completed."' No, it may not be possible. But we also have to remember that in the United States, where a much greater measure of justice was accorded to indigenes than is at present envisaged in Australia, Wounded Knee is about broken treaties, broken promises, dirty deals.

Once the most immediate material and social problems of blacks have been healed, there still looms the further problem that blacks continue to have to exist within the all-pervading, dominant framework of a white society. A lot of the dead wood has to be chipped off that framework, but the basic frame will still be there. This would be so even in a separate black state. I have already stressed the need for an *independent* black organisation that (parish-pump politics allowing) will unite the black people of Australia. Gordon Bryant on February 16, 1973 said that if a majority of Aborigines wanted a direct representation in federal parliament, he would support them (without necessarily considering it such a good idea at this stage). Of course a majority opinion is, at this time, an extremely difficult thing to obtain. Indeed there is not yet the machinery for it (and I mean in black organisational terms, *not* white). Perhaps we *do* need that monster conference ... and yes, perhaps the whole thing *is* a bit premature, despite the fact that we already have Senator Neville Bonner up there. It is important. In due course Aborigines must arrive at direct representation. They must take their place in the Australian parliament because that parliament will continue to have a bearing on their lives and is, therefore, of continuing significance. But we must not forget that a black face in parliament may mean nothing. He might be an imitation white man. We have seen this happening in the United States. If a black man in parliament is not an Aboriginal patriot possessed of real guts, he won't be of much use to the people.

Probably the toughest thing that blacks are going to have to come to grips with is their own psychological condition. Sure, the white man put you there, psychologically, but even if he wants to he can't get you out. Materially yes, psychologically, no. What then, are we going to do about the self-hatred that he has imposed upon us? You see it streaming out of every black speaker every time he opens his mouth. It is this self-hate that cripples so many black personalities. Some time ago Bob and Kaye Bellear had a six-year-old girl staying with them. This kid, from Cherbourg is 'going to be white' when she grows up. It is much better to be white. She can't understand how it is that Bob is black and yet not drunk. You can go almost anywhere in the south and see Aboriginal kids standing over one another demanding, 'Who are *you* calling black?' 'Bla . . hh . . ck' — it's almost an expletive. Such is the conditioning.

Many blacks are afraid of success. Failure they understand, failure they expect, failure they know how to react to. You see blacks who have considerable intellect and ability dodging responsibility because they fear to draw attention to themselves. They don't really believe they are as good as whites and they fear their competition. That is why a Mundine or a Goolagong or a Lionel Rose is so important to blacks — especially if they have the grace to identify first and foremost as Aborigines, *not* as Australians. That too, is why the rejection of white control, white values and all 'whiteness' is such an important part of a move back to black pride.

Aborigines have long hoped that integration, as distinct from assimilation, would allow them to interact with whites at a level of natural dignity. Of course the reality of integration, whatever it really means, is less glorious. Whites are never quite natural with you and how can you integrate except as equals? Always there is some degree of over-compensation, some tokenism, some paternalism in white/black relations (except when you've bashed it out of one another in a marriage; artificial things don't survive *that* mill). While I don't believe that it is as bad here as it is in the USA, blacks nevertheless find that, amongst whites, they must prove their personal acceptability over and over again.

Both to whites and to themselves, they have to keep on proving it. Against these efforts looms a huge ogre — the Aboriginal racial stereotype — dirty, lazy, unreliable, bludging, shifty little 'Jacky'. This stereotyping applies not only to individuals but to black communities as well. So in the long run, individuals can't get free until the group gets free. Free of an attitude, free of a memory, free of a psychological set. And how is this achieved? I don't know, any more than I know why it is that at various times in my life, conditions notwithstanding, I have seen some blacks who *do* get through. Somehow these people have arrived at a point of security, a point of acceptance of themselves as valuable human beings. Usually these people have come to an understanding of their tribal antecedents, the spiritual content, and also have some ideas of social evolution and what constitutes truly *human* values. Pearl Gibbs put it this way, 'Black power, white power ... what about what I'm interested in, *human* power?' Or Malcolm X, 'We don't want to be integrationists. Nor do we want to be separationists. We want to be human beings.'

Because white people have not yet attained *their* full humanity, blacks must, of necessity, draw together and attempt to re-create each other without them. But still they will mix, the two races. Perhaps it was ordained, millennia ago, by whatever forces ordain these things that one day this country, this Australia would, because of the very nature of those who were drawn to live in it, come to see

> The human metals melt and melting down
> Strike fault in fault and shattering neath the steel
> The two base metals scream a new appeal.

Epilogue

It has become necessary, as I correct the proofs of this book late in September, to supply a final commentary on developments in Aboriginal affairs under the Labor government since the announcement of its provisions for blacks in the 1973–4 budget and the release of the interim report of the Woodward Commission at the end of July. The period between March and September has been one of increasing disillusionment for Aborigines. Everywhere you can hear them commenting that Labor talks good, promises a lot, but is proving to be just as accomplished at the ultimate side-step as its Liberal predecessors.

The 'land rights' that Gough Whitlam bestowed so magnificently in his policy speech are increasingly being found to have almost no relation to Aborigines' ideas of what land rights entail. And in every other sphere of white–black relations history is once again repeating itself under Labor. Once again, despite an impressive start, the promises are being revealed to have no real substance. Australia's Aborigines, except in odd showpiece areas such as at Wattie Creek and so on are *not* going to be given a land base; they are *not* going to be given compensation. And they are certainly not going to cease to be done to and done for by their white masters.

With black help, the Australian Union of Students not long ago released a special edition of its newspaper, *National U*, under the title *Black National U*. Points of special interest include:

1. The policy of the ALP is, in essence, the same as that of the last government. It too aims at the progressive integration and assimilation of Aborigines through the process of increased dependence on white institutions.
2. The National Aborigines' Consultative Committee will have no executive powers; is being forced upon the people; is alien to the Aboriginal mode of decision making; will act as a buffer for government as it implements policies that are adverse to blacks.
3. The NACC (and especially its non-urban representatives) will *depend* on black bureaucrats and others for direction and hence will be easily led by the various administrations and institutions which, through their multifarious forms of intimidation, can easily force and influence voting patterns to ensure a subservient conservative vote.
4. The NACC's white counterpart, the Council for Aboriginal Affairs, composed of Mr Dexter, Dr Coombs and Professor Stanner, can override any NACC recommendation.
5. The 1971 ALP Conference at Launceston stated in part that 'Aboriginal land rights shall carry with them full rights to minerals in those lands'. The ALP Conference held in Surfers Paradise in July 1973 replaced this with 'All Aborigines to share the benefit from the development of natural resources, including minerals, on Aboriginal lands'. This definitely shows that the *government* will ultimately decide just how national resources on black land will be exploited. Aboriginal rights then, will only exist in so far as they don't conflict with the needs of mining companies.
6. John Little, junior barrister assisting A. E. Woodward as defending counsel in the Yirrkala land case, has claimed (at a meeting of the International Commission of Jurists held earlier this year) that the case was lost even before it started because Woodward believed that the Yirrkala land *was* lost and knew that the Nabalco operation would not be stopped by the government even if by the flimsiest chance a decision was made in favour of land rights.

7. Woodward, Nabalco representatives, Dr Coombs (arguing for the Liberal government) and others had met in Sydney on September 26, 1969 to discuss a compromise proposal for compensation for the Yirrkala in return for the forfeiture of their land … behind the Yirrkala's backs!
8. The ALP has meant, in Aboriginal affairs, changes in *quantity,* not quality. However the only result of the increased spending will be increased dependency. It will also create a mammoth racist bureaucratic inertia too powerful to overcome as the Department of Aboriginal Affairs grows.
9. The only power Aborigines will ultimately have will be in their ability for political organisation *independent of the institutions of government.*

*

About the time that the above came out that excellent little information sheet *Black News* (No 5) commented that:

1. The budget allocation for Aboriginal affairs (meaning the white people who control Aboriginal affairs) will be used mainly for housing, the employment of more whites and to put Aboriginal people to sleep. It was not likely to be used for real development of the Aboriginal people.
2. Woodward's interim report does not recognise land rights on the basis of Aboriginal Law. It only allows some communities to control certain areas and then only on certain conditions.
3. Without waiting to see if the interim report has Aboriginal support or not, Bryant has announced that the government has accepted it and will act on it straightaway.
4. Money, mostly for the south, denial of land rights for the north, this seems to be the trick that Bryant and Woodward are trying to pull, even if they don't see it that way themselves … The point is, nothing basic has changed … *Bunji* (the newspaper of the Larrakia group in Darwin) pointed out that their estimate of the compensation required was not mentioned in Woodward's report. The report acknowledged not a

shred of guilt, not a hint of white thieving and consequent enrichment ... So much noise, little change, plenty of cash, no land rights.

*

In September an officer of the Department of Aboriginal Affairs contacted me to see if I would write an Aboriginal's reaction to the interim report and Labor's budgetary provisions for blacks. Apparently the Australian Information Service needed it for an Italian magazine which was planning to do a spread on the Aboriginal situation in Australia. I don't know whether the article ever got to whatever Italian magazine it was but my main points, as valid for this epilogue as for that article were:

1. It is clear that Labor *et al.* are going to stick to their 'land by traditional occupancy' guns. This will effectively cut off the majority of blacks' capacity to substantiate a land claim. All over the country, but especially in the south, detribalisation and deliberate policies of forced removal, assimilation, etc., by governments, administrations and missions over the generations have ensured that traditional links with the land in the sense that Woodward means it have been erased. All this is ignored. In other words, the more you've been ruined and disrupted, the less chance you're going to get to build a new life, even though your family might have lived in a place for as long as anyone can remember and even though your grandmother can still remember the day when grazier so and so finally got a long-term lease for land on which your people had lived for so much longer than that. Even in the Northern Territory you will find many Aboriginal groups that would be uphill proving traditional association with the land, let alone in the south.
2. John Little, Woodward's junior barrister, has claimed that he was prevented from putting what he regarded as a winning argument for land rights. (See *Retrieval* March/April 1973 p. 4.)
3. Basically the land rights question is one of who gets what as against who holds onto what and who pays for what —

inevitably a racial division. Within his carefully restricted terms of reference Woodward spins an ingenious web of words so as to classify Aboriginal land holding (which was a living, natural fact) according to white concepts which he can then use to disqualify most of Australia's blacks from achieving a place in the sun. So he disqualifies the Larrakia people of Darwin from land rights by means of a piece of sophistry that questions the length and extent of their attachment to the area they are claiming; it may have belonged to a different clan of their tribe! The crunch, of course, is the effect of the claim on Darwin's 'town planning considerations' and the 'possible effect on the rights of other persons [whites] who have already bought blocks of land in the area in good faith'. (This was known for a long time, yet the developers were not stopped. Also, both objections could be overcome with adequate money but that, apparently, is not considered.) A great deal of the report is concerned with a discussion of the potential difficulties that land rights would raise for the *white man.* Like the *Gove Land Rights* case, it boils down to an exercise in sophistry, not an investigation into real human possibilities.

4. Mining is a touchy subject. Should Aborigines, wonders Justice Woodward, be allowed to decide against mineral exploitation on their land, so subverting the 'national interest'? How much is the blacks' share to be ... considering the need to keep the incentives for whites up? Should the government search for minerals? If so and minerals are found, should blacks be allowed to veto the results of a search? (There are no prizes for the nearest correct answer.)
5. On August 22, 1973 Mr Bryant announced that the government had accepted the major recommendations of the report. He intends to proceed immediately with the preparation of draft legislation for the incorporation of Aboriginal communities and groups without waiting for the final report next year. Land is to be vested in communities once they have been incorporated. *Blacks are at a crossroads in their history on this matter.* On no account must they fall into the error of

allowing land to be vested in small groups or clans, for to do so will make them an easy target in the future. It only takes one drunk or one fool or one traitor to sell the land forever. Whites will have the land back within a generation and will have robbed the Aborigines of any moral basis for a new land claim. It is a policy of divide and conquer. *All land must be granted in perpetuity, be vested in a National Aboriginal Land Trust for the Aboriginal people as a whole and be incapable of alienation.* Local groups would have special rights within this broad framework. All mining should be reserved according to Aborigines' wishes.

6. The Woodward report talks vaguely about grants (government administered) for black developments. But it expressly denies the principle of monetary compensation for Aborigines. The question of compensation is not in his terms of reference and that is that, no matter how integral a part of the general land claim it is.
7. The NACC is to afford 'black consultation'. In fact, everything will be done according to the white man's values, definitions, structures and (ultimately) interests. The election is a fiasco. The elected representatives will be in no way representatives in fact. Not enough time was given for the elections to be conducted at all properly and they were easily 'steered' by interested whites and blacks (as I have shown in articles elsewhere). The 'election' was not carried out according to the Aboriginal way and overrides existing black leadership patterns. Another 'being done to'!
8. White people are thoroughly impressed, no doubt, with the allocation of $117 million for black affairs this budget. My point is that $50 million spent according to black needs as determined by blacks will yield much more in terms of meaningful development than $117 million used according to white determination. This fact is explained by the same set of psychological determinants that ensure that if a white voluntary body or a government erects a hall or whatever on an Aboriginal reserve and forgets to erect high protective fencing, the windows and walls will be guaranteed to be stoned

and broken within twelve months. Blacks do not consider that it is 'ours' — as indeed it isn't. Anything imposed upon them by whites, no matter how well intentioned it may be, will inevitably go the same way. If however, a hall were to be desired, planned for and *achieved* by the people according to their own wishes (and at their own pace, however slow) and built with their own sweat, then it wouldn't be stoned. That is the vital difference between 'being done to' and real human growth. That explains why $50 million *black* is worth much more than $117 million white.

9. Then of course there is the question of how the money is to be channelled. How much is to go to projects that blacks would never let black money be used for? How much is to go in salaries for public service fat cats? How much to benefit whites?

*

Where can blacks turn? To whom can they appeal? Where do you appeal, after all, when you know that the thief is the judge? Like its predecessors, Labor is essentially concerned with the application of band-aids, bigger and better though they are. But the essential thing, *the challenge of the regeneration of a race*, is not accepted. *Black National U* recommends that 'the only power Aborigines will ultimately have will be in their ability for political organisation independent of the institutions of government'. Chapter 12 of this book gives an outline of the reasons why this is so difficult for blacks at this time. So what is left? Frustration, negation, blind hatred, powerlessness … the psychological nadir. Where can blacks go, in Australia today, except to Chapter 7?

